Blossom

Adriana Picker

Blossom

PRACTICAL AND CREATIVE WAYS TO FIND
WONDER IN THE FLORAL WORLD

Hardie Grant

BOOKS

Contents

Summer 125

Introduction

My life is punctuated by plants – small cycles I mentally track so as not to miss the fleeting cloud of wisteria perfume in spring, or the opportunity to walk through freshly fallen gingko leaves in autumn. The word 'human' comes from the Greek *humus*: we as people are literally of the earth, hewn from the soil beneath our feet. But our lives are so intertwined with the plant kingdom that it's easy to take this for granted.

In Japan, the calendar is split into seventy-two micro-seasons, offering a poetic journey through the year in which the land awakens, blooming with life and activity before returning to slumber. This concept resonated strongly with me when I stumbled upon it, because I realised that this is how I live my life – the greater movement of the seasons is shattered into a thousand smaller movements. Tiny cycles and changes tell me when to start watching for the first determined crocus to poke through the snow as winter yields to spring, or when the first precocious buds of *Magnolia stellata* will begin to unfurl. I wait with bated breath every year for the first heady, fragrant flush of lilac in spring; or the gentle autumn rain and stop of cold that brings the generous saffron milk cap mushroom, which really cannot be purchased, only searched for among pine trees and picked with your own hands. I would cancel any plans or obligations for the privilege of listening closely to the rituals of the natural world.

Gardening and plants are part of my family history and DNA, a passion shared with my mother, aunt and grandmother. I grew up in the nineties, claustrophobic in a small town adjacent to the country with dial-up internet and no mobile phone, but I had a pony and great big fields to explore. I was aware of the laws and rhythms of plants. Still, I lusted for the city, for art and movement and revelry. And so I left for Sydney and didn't think about plants or the seasons until I came to realise how much I missed them – how much I was a part of them.

When I moved to New York in 2016, I was astounded to discover that the cycle of the seasons still existed within the confines of this concrete jungle. Not only did plants exist, they seemed amplified by their confines. I remember the single pot holding a vivacious rose tucked next to the trash cans, and the unwieldy geranium squeezed onto a stoop. Between the brownstones and the skyscrapers I found an unexpected botanical education, and with it connection and meaning in a new city. I was arrested by the deep, verdant greens in the vegetation thriving everywhere. The strips of nature in Australia are so often sunburnt and dry.

I started to create a mental map of places to visit regularly, irrespective of the season: the tiny West Village parks tended so proudly by neighbourhood volunteers; the incredible High Line; the Brooklyn Heights Promenade; the East Village parks; and of course the mother of them all, Central Park, cultivated not only for personal pleasure but also the joy and health of the collective. I learned the names of the trees and plants around me as a way of making New York home. I would repeat them under my breath as I walked: Callery pear, Kanzan cherry, *Iris reticulata*. It was a simple meditation that brought me into the present moment and centred me. Every time I found a new plant in an unfamiliar neighbourhood, it felt like a little piece of New York magic. My world crept outwards, plant by plant, inch by inch, until places no longer felt foreign. To find myself, I needed to find the flowers.

Then the Covid-19 pandemic happened. As I rushed to relocate back to my home country, Australia, I was forced to question and re-evaluate how I wanted to spend my time. What type of life did I want to lead? The overwhelming answer was a life closer to nature, consuming less and using my hands to make more. I wanted to interact with nature in a tactile and meaningful way.

So I sewed and dried and boiled and baked. I shaped clay and foraged for edible weeds and plunged my hands into the soil. I discovered more about herbal medicines, plant dyes, floral perfumes, seed saving, edible flowers, gardens that attract pollinators, preserving, fermenting, pickling, floral anatomy, and the history, mythology and language of plants. The journey to weave more flowers into my life was underway.

Plants have been my landmarks when life became turbulent. They have been stalwarts in precarious times, things I reached for to stay attached to solid ground. I know plants and they know me.

People have seasons, too, and it cannot always be spring. When I have been too burnt out to draw, I have sewn fig leaves into quilts, and I have cooked them to make ricotta from their magical sap. I have sought out the nature lovers of the world and found solace in their company. The poet Mary Oliver has been a perennial friend; she wrote in nature while walking, creating moving meditations observed by the eyes of an artist. Her poems speak of roses singing, and being saved by the beauty of the world. The masterful Robin Wall Kimmerer writes of the songs of flowers, too, and the ancient knowledge of entering into a state of reciprocity with the natural world. My friends are florists and artists inspired by flowers; we speak the same language and have been bitten by the same bug.

This book is a map for your own botanical journey, an antidote
to the disconnecting forces of technology and modern society.
It's about understanding the natural world, caring for it and
taking pleasure in it, whether you're in a city apartment, the
suburbs or the country. The words and illustrations found
within these pages are my attempt to turn our attention to the
detailed, growing and ever-changing beauty of the plant world.
Flowers offer us a way to observe and defer to the nuances
of the seasons, and they're a balm for the overtaxed mind.
They are not reliant on dates but divided by micro-seasons
and fleeting moments: when the first cherry blossom appears,
when milk thistle goes to seed. Let this book be your guide
to cultivating a new curiosity about the rhythms of nature,
and deepen your understanding of how to live by them. Find
wonder in common things; it's extraordinary what grows in
the crack of a pavement if you care to look. Listen to the roses
sing; hear what they are saying to you. Fall in love with the
wonder of the everyday, and be saved like Mary Oliver, like
me, by the beauty of the world.

Spring

Chinese magnolia

MAGNOLIA × SOULANGEANA ———————— MAGNOLIACEAE

The blossoms of the magnolia tree began gracing spring with their beauty over 95 million years ago, giving it the distinction of being one of the first angiosperms, or flowering plants. This ancient genus, which fossil records suggest is from the Cretaceous period, tells tales of drifting continents, the rise of mountains and the extinction of dinosaurs. The endurance of this plant family can be matched by few others; only ginkgoes, conifers and cycads dominated the landscape before magnolias.

For such an elegant flower, magnolia can be considered 'primitive' in botanical circles. The durable blooms are thought to have evolved to encourage pollination by beetles and can withstand their blundering search for nectar, quite different from the delicate dance of a bee. At night, the blooms close to trap the beetles inside in a pollen-rich stupor until morning.

I did not think I could possibly love magnolia blossoms more, and then I discovered that they are edible and taste sweetly of ginger. The lovely fuzzy buds can also be used to make a tea that is reported to help indigestion, but personally I would feel very sad to pick a bud before it had the chance to burst into glorious bloom.

The 'precocious' children of the magnolia family – those that dare to share their beauty with the world in early spring, without the protection of leaves – are my kind. A burst of dramatic colour tethered to gnarled, bare branches, blooms waltzing with the wind like the painterly wings of enormous butterflies, decorating even the most humdrum streetscapes with a frosting of pastel pink, magenta or lemon yellow. And when the petals melt into the pavement, they remind our hearts to rejoice at the resilience of tender things. If a magnolia blossom can survive an ice age, we can leave behind the winter gloom and step bravely into spring.

Pickled magnolia petals

My favourite use for magnolia petals is to pickle them in a light vinegar brine to use in place of pickled ginger in salads, sushi and stir-fries.

Clean and dry 300–350 g (10½–12¼ oz/6–7 cups) of young magnolia petals, being careful not to bruise them (they brown quickly after being cut so I prefer to pickle them whole). Add to sterilised jars, packed tightly. Heat around 500 ml (17 fl oz/2 cups) vinegar (I use honey-like persimmon vinegar, but apple cider vinegar would work also) with 300 g (10½ oz /1⅓ cups) sugar and 2 teaspoons salt, and simmer until dissolved. Add some black peppercorns or star anise if you'd like to enhance the flavour of your pickle. Pour the hot brine over the petals. Submerge the petals as much as possible, then pop the jars into the fridge and let sit overnight.

This quick pickle is not shelf stable so should be stored in the fridge and used within 2 weeks.

Eastern redbud

CERCIS CANADENSIS ———————— FABACEAE

**The eastern redbud announces the arrival of spring
in a unique and extraordinary fashion that cannot
be ignored. Clusters of small dark-red buds and then
soft pink, magenta or white flowers burst directly
from its furrowed trunk and zigzagging branches – a
characteristic known as cauliflory, more common in
rainforest plants such as cacao, coffee and papaya. This
small but generous tree, a member of the legume family,
only reaches 6 to 9 metres (20 to 30 ft) tall but can carry
an abundance of 20,000 flowers. Blossoming before the
leaves appear allows pollinators to reach the flowers
more successfully, and creates an other-worldly display
that looks too wildly sculptural to be real, like the blooms
have infested the host tree with an unnatural beauty.**

Redbud flowers attract a range of bees and butterflies,
especially bees with longer tongues, such as carpenter and
blueberry bees; shorter-tongued bees cannot reach the nectar.
The leaves (bronze at first then a verdant lime green) are
favourites with leafcutter bees, whose perfect circles of leaf are
carried off as nesting material, leaving telltale cut-out patterns
behind. In autumn the leaves flush a startling crimson (most
appropriate for their heart shape) then fall, leaving papery
seed pods rustling on bare branches. The seed pods are shaped
like a weaver's shuttle, and the name *Cercis* derives from the
Greek word for this, *kerkis*.

Cercis canadensis is found across central–eastern North America, but a sister species grows along the west coast, and another in the Middle East. It's the latter that earned the redbud its other common name – the Judas tree. Legend has it that Judas Iscariot, after betraying Jesus, chose to hang himself from a *Cercis*. Until then, all these trees were tall, upright and strong, bearing white flowers, but afterwards the tree became twisted and bent, its wood brittle, and its flowers blushed pink with shame.

America's First Nations people found medicinal and other uses for the plant, including dyes and basketry. The flowers, young pods and leaves are edible, with a sweet acidic taste, but flowers from similar-looking plants can be poisonous, so it's important never to eat anything you cannot fully identify.

A redbud by any other name

We become familiar with plants by learning their names. We want to claim them. Most plants have a common name that is easy to pronounce and remember. However, this can pose a problem because many different plants can have the same common name, and sometimes one plant can have several. For example, *Alliaria petiolata*, a flowering plant in the mustard (Brassicaceae) family, is known by the common name penny hedge, jack-in-the-bush, garlic root, poor man's mustard, hedge garlic, sauce-alone or garlic mustard, depending on where you are in the world. To avoid confusion, each plant is given a scientific, or botanical, name.

Latin was the language used for the first recorded categorisation of plants in around 400 BCE. Nearly two millennia later, Swedish naturalist and explorer Carl Linnaeus organised plants into twenty-four distinct families, grouping them by physical appearance. Although most of Linnaeus's classifications are now out of date, his legacy endures through binomial nomenclature, a practice of assigning two-part names to each species, and Latin is still used. The first word, which is always capitalised, denotes the genus of the plant, and the second word, which is always lower case, usually suggests the plant's characteristics, indicates its species and can be very poetic – the stories behind these names are frequently magical. The names of the plant families share a suffix: -aceae.

But the naming of plants in scientific Latin is not without problems – it is interwoven with the history of colonialism and the erosion of Indigenous cultures and traditional knowledge around the world. Why should the Australian banksia, known to the First Peoples of Australia for more than 80,000 years, be named after the Englishman Joseph Banks who 'discovered' it some 200 years ago?

Modern technological and scientific advances have enabled taxonomists to look at the DNA of a plant to determine how and when it evolved. While many gene-sequencing studies have confirmed classifications accepted by botanists for centuries, surprises are not uncommon and errors are continually uncovered. Hostas are no longer considered to be related to lilies, and now belong to the Asparagaceae family, along with agave, hyacinth and bluebells. Rosemary, once *Rosmarinus officinalis*, is now called *Salvia rosmarinus* after it was found to be more closely related to sage than previously thought. Whole plant families have been eliminated entirely. But sometimes a name change is inconsequential, especially to the layperson; a rose is still simply a rose and smells just as sweet.

Border forsythia

FORSYTHIA × INTERMEDIA ——————— OLEACEAE

For those living in cold climates where midwinter feels bleak and endless, there is much joy in witnessing a large bush become covered in masses of luminous yellow four-petalled flowers in early spring. Forsythia, which is in the same family as olives, is one of the first garden plants to bloom on still-bare stems, with bright green leaves following as the great shocks of yellow flowers fade.

All but one species of forsythia comes from East Asia, and their bushy growth provides good cover for nesting birds. Bees must also rejoice at this early respite from desolate winter – they are forsythia's main pollinator, but interestingly cannot enjoy the golden display as we do, as they only see red, blue, green and ultraviolet light. Many blooms have ultraviolet patterning, invisible to our gaze, that guide insects to a pollen lunch like tiny landing lights.

Early blooms

If you cut a few long stems of forsythia (or other early blooms) once the buds have started to swell, you can enjoy an even earlier treat indoors, where the warmth will 'force' the flowers to open sooner – although it might take a week or two. Place the stems in water, removing any buds that are submerged; keep trimming the stems and changing the water regularly to avoid rotting.

Three-cornered garlic

ALLIUM TRIQUETRUM ——————— AMARYLLIDACEAE

These pretty little flowers are my seasonal clock; I take heed of their brief flowering season, as it is a harbinger of many other much-anticipated botanical occurrences. Clusters of white flowers droop down the stems they are named after (break them and you will find a perfect triangle Pythagoras would lust after), each petal decorated by a single elegant green stripe, their smell a mere whiff of their more ubiquitous cousins.

A member of the *Allium* genus well known by foraging enthusiasts, the whole plant – bulb, leaves and flowers – can be eaten, but the delicate ephemeral flowers are the prize for me. Native to the Mediterranean Basin, three-cornered garlic is an invasive weed in many places and can have a serious impact on natural habitats – by eating the enemy you are doing nature a good turn. I have foraged them in damp pockets right near Sydney's iconic Bronte Beach, and I love adding their subtle garlicky flavour to omelettes or blending a pesto to run through some unctuous fresh pasta.

Tempura flowers

Many other flowers would work well as a substitute in this light-as-air tempura – as would any other allium – but I think the delicate flavour of three-cornered garlic is particularly delicious.

Whisk together 150 g (5¼ oz/1 cup) sifted 00 flour (minimising gluten will keep the batter light), 300 ml (10¼ fl oz/1¼ cup) chilled sparkling water, 1 egg and a pinch of table salt. Pour a neutral oil into a large frying pan to about 5 cm (2 in) in depth, and gently heat the oil to around 180° (356°F). Coat 220 g (7¾ oz/4⅓ cups) three-cornered garlic flowers and stems in batter, and then fry them in batches for about 30 seconds on each side (it does not take long at all!). You want them to be crispy but not golden. Once the tempura flowers are cooked, place them on kitchen paper to absorb the excess oil, and then enjoy without delay.

Lilac

SYRINGA VULGARIS —————— OLEACEAE

It is not the beautiful sight of lilac's namesake-coloured blossoms that first assaults the senses but its intoxicating perfume, wafting around city blocks and down country lanes alike. When lilac is in bloom I will make any number of detours to plunge my nose into blossoms – an olfactory adventure that taunts with joyful memories of springs past.

Picked first thing in the morning for millennia, while the dew still clings to its petals and its fragrance is at its height, delicate lilac does not fare well with contemporary perfume methods. To produce a true perfume from lilac is a labour of love and ancient tradition. We delve into this process, called enfleurage, on pages 136–7. Edible lilac also makes a beautiful aromatic contribution to drinks and desserts.

In contrast to the delicate nature of its scent, the lilac plant – a member of the olive family – is enduring and hardy once established. An ancient shrub reportedly planted by Thomas Jefferson in the 1700s is still in flower today at his plantation, Monticello, Virginia. Lilac was also planted across the United States to honour Abraham Lincoln after his death in 1865, inspired by a commemorative poem by Walt Whitman.

The common lilac won't open its buds until it is safe to do so, which is why the flowering may vary by as much as three weeks from one season to another. It has long been recognised as a reliable indicator plant – used by farmers to predict events like the warming of the soil, temperature and humidity. Phenological calendars were used by the ancient Romans and Chinese, but sadly lilacs are now an important indicator of climate change. This idea of marking the passage of time by slowing down to be in rhythm with nature seems a valuable lesson to learn.

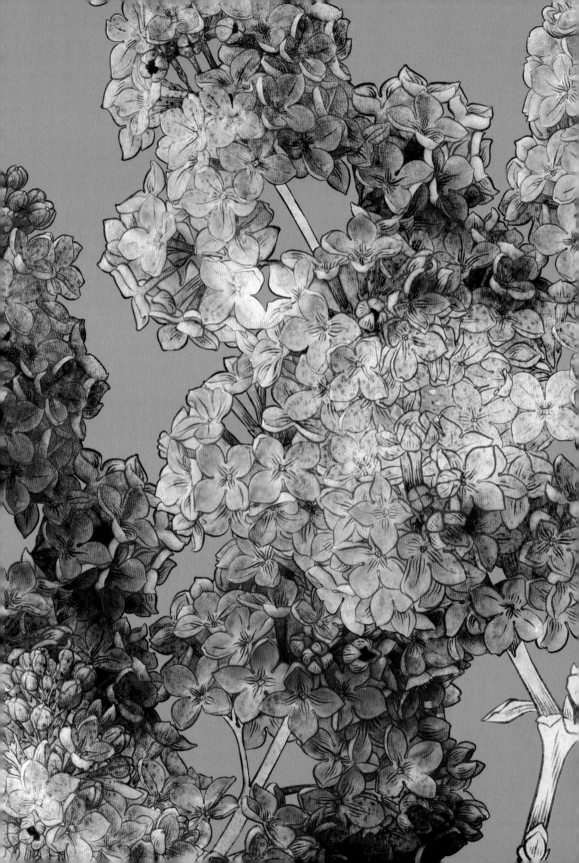

Lilac vinegar

Making vinegar from the natural yeasts found on blossoms is a magical age-old process that preserves the ephemeral flavours of spring for enjoyment all year round. Lilac lends a lemony, floral essence to this apple cider vinegar. Just add soda water (club soda) for a delicious mocktail or a splash of gin for a delicious cocktail. I have also enjoyed making floral wine vinegar – replacing the apple juice with a light white wine and avoiding the need for the first fermentation.

Though rather simple, this method can take some experimentation to master. For ease you can always start the process with the addition of commercial yeast – dried champagne yeast is best.

The first part of the process is the fermentation of juice into alcohol. Add 4 litres (roughly 1 gallon) of apple juice and 50–100 g (1¾–3½ oz/1–2 cups) of lilac blossoms, removed from their stems, to a large jar. Stir well. Cover the jar with a cloth and secure with a string or rubber band to keep out pests, and place in a cool position as this is best for wild yeast growth.

Ferment for 7–14 days to let the alcohol develop. Oxygen benefits this ferment, so stirring once or twice a day will speed up the process. Wild yeasts are slow starters, so do not expect bubbles to form quickly. Make sure the flower petals remain submerged so they don't spoil and ruin the flavour of the ferment. Once ready, it should smell sweet, fruity and slightly alcoholic.

The second part of the process is making vinegar from the alcohol. Pour 250 ml (8½ fl oz/1 cup) (or roughly 20 per cent of the weight of the juice) unpasteurised raw apple cider vinegar into your jar. It's not essential, but you can also add a small piece of vinegar mother (try finding one online from a Buy Nothing group). Re-cover the vinegar and place it in a warm spot to encourage a new mother to grow over top of the liquid, which will protect the vinegar and its flavours as it ferments.

Check the vinegar in a month – if it is sweet and slightly bubbly, fermentation is still occurring and it may take another month or two to fully develop. Once ready, strain out the mother and blossoms and pour the vinegar into a sterilised bottle with as little air as possible, then store it in the fridge. Save the mother for another batch or share it with a friend.

A wide range of flowers make delicious vinegars and impart their own unique characters. Try roses, lavender, chive blossoms (or any other allium), elderflower, rosemary, sage or even an edible variety of wattle. Make sure your selection is definitely edible and has been grown without pesticides that would kill the wild yeast – not to mention be toxic.

Tulip

TULIPA × GESNERIANA ——————— LILIACEAE

My obsession with tulips flourished when I moved to New York in 2016. The city's long love affair with the tulip began with the arrival of the Dutch East India Company in the 1600s, during a golden age for the Dutch that paved the way for grand explorations and floral follies. Now, during April and May, New York is literally blanketed in them. There are millions of blooms planted over the five boroughs, with 70,000 planted along Park Avenue alone. Their overwhelming presence is the perfect antidote to the often grey and rainy New York spring.

Tulips are not as likely to re-bloom as daffodils (they also fall prey to squirrels, who dig them up for dinner), so they are most often replanted each year and thus treated as temporary installations (and a serious investment) for spring celebrations.

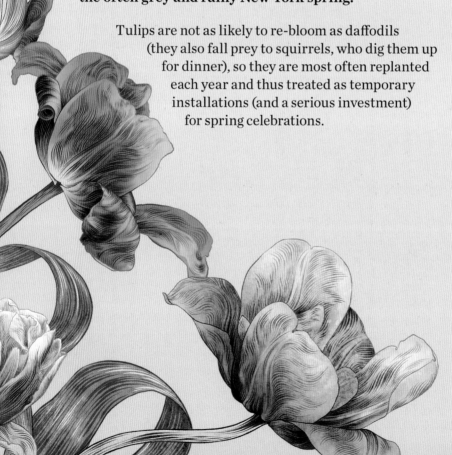

It was the 'flamed' tulip varieties that produced what is now considered the first speculative investment bubble: 'tulip mania'. The most valuable bulbs were those that produced multicoloured petals, a rare phenomenon caused by a virus. During this period, some single bulbs sold for more than ten times the annual income of a skilled labourer. The term 'tulip mania' is still used metaphorically in trading circles to reference a serious deviation from trading value. I can't help but love the idea of a flower – all her beauty reflected in her unpredictability – being so highly valued.

These complex multicoloured blooms, alive with movement, are simply begging to be eternalised. The Dutch masters knew this, using them as the muse of countless masterpieces. Tulips are also the subject of many of my drawings. I love watching them bend and reach for the light in a vase, the form of the blooms perfect for my linework.

The glorious swaths of a bed planted in a single colour of tulips is a welcome sight on early spring days, awakening the senses after months of monotonous city winter. But, for me, coming across a multicoloured bloom is particularly exciting – it will always be in her imperfections that nature is the most perfect.

How to see like an artist

I think my love of minute detail has made me the artist I am. I've spent an inordinate amount of time looking at flowers – countless hours, including most of my adult life and a vast portion of my childhood.

I encourage you to observe a plant as closely as possible – the veins on a leaf, the whorls on a petal – and see what unexpected joys of discovery abound. How closely have you observed a flower? Botanists and horticulturalists keep loupes stashed in their pockets, ever ready to observe a blossom or leaf or stamen.

An artist does this, too. To make a beautiful artwork – to solidify the ever-changing, the ephemeral onto the page – I believe the work is broken up equally into that of our hands and that of our eyes, our ways of seeing and observing. The object we see and what our unpractised minds want us to record on the page are two vastly different things. Our minds want to find pattern and symmetry and order; we fill in the gaps of hurried observation with similarities and repetition. This is how we make sense of the world, but an artist must resist this compulsion with every fibre of their being.

The real beauty of nature is in the flaws: the wild, the broken and the messy. It is in the curl of a crushed leaf, the unpredictable holes chomped by a famished caterpillar, the imperfect, the unschooled, the stunted. The eye calibrates with practice and looks for these perfect imperfections, and the hand marks them on a page. Hundreds and thousands of hours of observation tune the eye to look for stress cracks in petals, the gradient of sunburn that fades a dark purple leaf to tan and the great variation between the size and shape of fig leaves on the same tree.

This will be a lifelong pursuit for me, an increasingly deeper dive into the joy of simple, everyday discovery and the quest for more and more detail. This is how we learn to ask many unanswerable questions, like how to draw the innumerable filaments of a mimosa blossom.

Apple blossom

MALUS SYLVESTRIS ——————— ROSACEAE

My journey into the botanical world has been filled with
many surprises, both large and small. One discovery that
astonished me is how the humble apple tree is a close cousin
of the rose, the strawberry bush and the plum tree. How could
these plants, seemingly so diverse in character, be related?
I now find great joy in mentally cataloguing their similarities
and pondering how evolution has put them on such divergent
paths. I love to note that the petals of a strawberry flower
are reflected in the same gentle shape of an old-fashioned
climbing rose or a crabapple. The branches of a pear tree may
tower high above the canes of a raspberry, but the tiny notches
in their leaves correspond. Familial traits passed down over
the ages, just like your great-grandmother's long forehead or
weak ankles.

Close observation of a cluster of apple blossoms will reveal a
distinct pattern. The pink buds form in clusters of six, with five
buds surrounding one centre bud called the king blossom. The king
blossom is larger and opens its delicate white petals first; the others
follow suit, one at a time. If all goes to plan, this vulnerable act of
blossoming will produce fruit after pollination. Apple seeds (called
pippins – how cute!) produce genetically divergent plants from their
parent trees – referred to as heterozygotes – meaning the Granny
Smith variety, for example, is a clone of the parent tree from a
cutting grafted on rootstock.

Apple blossoms are edible and they have a sweet, fragrant flavour
that lends well to syrups, wild fermented sodas and garnishes.
I couldn't think of anything lovelier than a cloud of apple blossoms
adorning a cake.

Introduction to scent extraction

The synthesised scents of flowers are ubiquitous in contemporary life. They embellish our sunscreens, soaps, shampoos and even our dishwashing liquids. We want to adorn ourselves with the allure of flowers, we want to cover ourselves in their scents. The desire to exude a floral aroma is not unique to modern times. Scent was holy in the ancient world and used in the worship of gods. The ancient Egyptians were passionate perfumers, and the ancient Romans and Greeks burned incense to swathe their environs in aroma. The word 'perfume' has its roots in the Latin *per fumus*, meaning through smoke, and medieval Europeans believed fragrance prevented disease. Throughout history, humans have displayed a consistent inclination to smell like flowers. Although blossoms exude pleasant scent naturally, perfumes are deliberate creations of human ingenuity. Perfumers meticulously employ their knowledge and skills to craft scents that surpass the offerings of nature, creating olfactory pleasures that delight the senses.

Four basic methods of scent extraction explored in this book are: infusing, using cold oil (the oldest and simplest method of infusing, requiring the least equipment, and what we will start with here); tincturing, using high-proof alcohol (page 60); distillation, using water and heat (page 53); and enfleurage, using solid fat or hot oil (pages 136–7).

Before you begin any process of scent extraction there are a few simple steps you need to follow to ensure you get the best perfume possible out of your flowers.

- Do your research and harvest your flowers when their scent is at its height. For example the perfume of lilac is most compelling in the early hours of the morning, whereas elderflower exudes the most sweetness on a warm day – if the bees are attracted by the aroma it is time to pick.

- Promptly prepare your flowers after harvesting for best results and avoid harvesting during rain.

- Gently wilting your blossoms is crucial, especially for infusions, as oil does not have the disinfecting qualities of an alcohol solvent and the water content can cause them to degrade rather quickly. Cover a cooling or oven rack with an absorbent cloth and place your flowers on this for a short time. Use your senses to monitor the flower's appearance and texture during wilting. They should become slightly limper but not lose their colour or spoil.

- Hygiene is very important in perfumery. It's essential to sterilise the jars and any equipment you plan to use to avoid contamination. You can do this by placing your glass jars in a hot oven for about 15 minutes and washing your utensils in high-proof perfumer's alcohol. Regularly check your infusions for signs of mould or decomposition. Infused fragrant oil has various uses, such as in candle making, soaps, bath salts, body oils, perfumes and even cleaning products.

Gently fill a jar halfway with wilted flowers (perhaps apple blossoms). Add oil (I generally use jojoba) until it covers all the petals and gently press down with a wooden spoon to release any trapped air that might encourage bacteria to grow. Take care not to shake the jar to avoid creating bubbles. Seal the jar and check it regularly to make sure the petals are submerged. If any water leaches from the plant material and forms a layer at the bottom of the jar, siphon off the oil. When the petals lose their vibrancy remove them from the oil and refresh it with new petals. Continue repeating the infusion until the desired aroma strength is achieved. Your infusion will generally be ready in 1–2 weeks.

Sweet violet

VIOLA ODORATA —————— VIOLACEAE

Violets are tender, discreet flowers that have hooked into the human spirit. For millennia they have been tied to myths, legends and fairytales. Beloved by the ancient Greeks and Shakespeare, the dark purple sweet or Eurasian violet, *Viola odorata*, is known for its sugary scent. Few other violets produce a noticeable fragrance.

The scent of the sweet violet possesses a certain kind of magic, which can literally avail us of our senses – or our sense of smell at least. The chemical compound that gives violets their sweet, powdery smell is called ionone, and it stimulates our scent receptors and then binds to them, briefly rendering us unable to detect the smell. The enchanting scent is there one moment and gone the next, only to reappear later, more powerful than before – a very clever illusionist's trick.

A bewitching bouquet of sweet violets was the romantic Napoleon Bonaparte's traditional gift to Empress Josephine each year on their anniversary. After thirteen years, Napoleon divorced Josephine and married a younger woman to ensure an heir, but his supporters adopted the violet as a symbol of loyalty to their leader. When Napoleon lay on his deathbed, his hand clutched a pendant filled with a lock of hair and dried violets. The last word that passed his lips was reportedly his true love's name – Josephine.

Violet mousse

This delectable dessert, garnished with fresh violets, serves 6. Begin by melting 300 g (10½ oz/2 cups) of dark chocolate in a bowl over gentle simmering water. In a separate bowl, whip 300 ml (10¼ fl oz/1¼ cup) thick cream (double/heavy) and chill. Heat 60 ml (2 fl oz/¼ cup) violet simple syrup (follow recipe for Wisteria syrup on page 69 and replace wisteria with violets) gently so as not to destroy the delicate aroma, then add 3 room-temperature egg yolks and whisk until pale and doubled in volume. Gently fold the whipped cream into the melted chocolate, then fold in the egg-yolk mixture. Chill until set before serving.

You could substitute violet simple syrup for rose or orange blossom simple syrup in this recipe with beautiful results.

Cherry blossom

PRUNUS SERRULATA 'KANZAN' —————— ROSACEAE

To lie under a tree in blossom is a fleeting spring gift of stillness and joy. The ancients dreamed of cherry blossoms and mourned their departure, just as we do: the *Prunus* genus can be traced back millions of years. The oldest tree of the genus still standing, the wild *Prunus x subhirtella*, has thrived in Japan for over 2000 years. Cherry blossoms are a common motif in ancient and contemporary Japanese poetry. As the waka poet Ariwara no Narihira wrote, 'If there were no cherry blossoms in this world / How much more tranquil our hearts would be in spring.'

I love all the wildly decorative cherries, but it is the double-petalled Kanzan that truly has my heart. (Honourable mention goes to the darling weeping cherry – who could not love strings of blossoms generously drooping to meet you.) In the distance a Kanzan is one shade of vibrant pink, a huge cloud fluttering against the eggshell-blue sky. The Kanzan viewed from below, however, makes for my favourite type of meditation.

Each year I lived in New York, I took a day off to picnic and lie underneath the cherry trees of Central Park. I would look up through the landscape of petals and uncountable hues of pink appearing in the depths. The blossoms twirled and whirled like a dancer's skirt, the ubiquitous jazz of a busker floating softly through the breeze of Central Park to keep her moving. I tried to name all the shades of pink I could see – the blush pink of a ballet slipper, the subtle pink of a van Gogh rose, the pink of Giambattista Valli, the pink of Wes Anderson. This meditation grounded me, like the cloud of a tree, lightly and gently to the here and now.

Glorious peak blossoms only last for a few brief weeks; a gust of wind or flurry of raindrops can end the transient reign of the Kanzan, and petals coat pavements, garden beds and tender grass with a *sakura* snow. The cherry blossom reminds us that beauty, like ourselves, is resilient, capable of rebirth each spring.

Bloom watch

Cherry blossom bud burst is a highly anticipated event each spring, and not just in Japan – it is beloved and eagerly awaited across the world. There are six stages in the cherry blossom blooming cycle, which, when closely watched, allow you to predict when their beauty will peak. The stages begin when green round buds appear as the weather warms up after winter. Next visible florets appear, then comes the extension of the florets. The peduncles elongate, and then fluffy petals start to appear. The climax of the stages comes when the tree is in peak bloom and full beauty. The first stage can last a long time, so it is more accurate to predict stages two to six, which take place across approximately twenty days. The cherry blossom tree becomes a floral clock of sorts, counting down the days until maximum botanic delight.

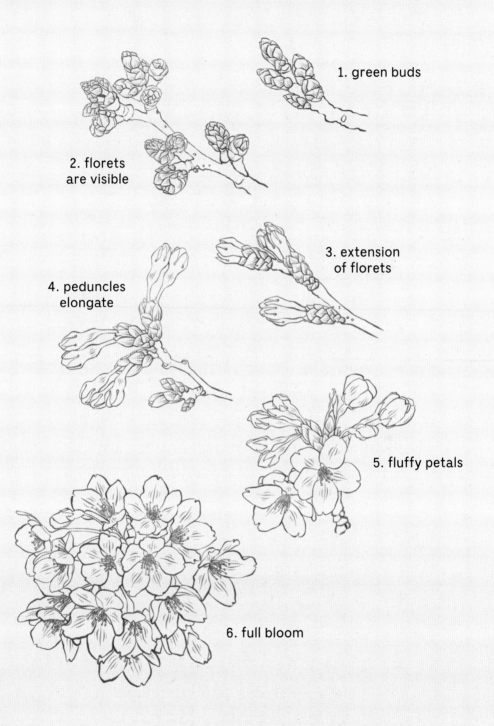

1. green buds

2. florets are visible

3. extension of florets

4. peduncles elongate

5. fluffy petals

6. full bloom

Rose

ROSA SPP. —————— ROSACEAE

The rose is the one flower universally recognised, perpetually popular and most imbued with meaning. My lifelong obsession with the glorious rose began in my grandmother's humble backyard.

The contemporary roses so popular today are descendants of 150 species of wild rose native to the northern hemisphere, with a particular abundance hailing from China. Rose breeders have been tinkering with that wild perfection for generations. The astonishing number of rose hybrids is testament to an almost fanatical quest for the botanically sublime – bolder blooms, a more intoxicating scent, a most perfect shade of pink. All hybrid varieties share the same lineage, being the progeny of crosses between either Gallicas, Damask roses or albas (I've drawn Damask on page 52, along with apothecary and Provence). A love for these old-fashioned varieties, I find, is the telltale sign of a true rose devotee.

It is the greatest of honours to have a rose hybrid named after you. There are roses named for royalty, politicians and sultry actresses like Brigitte Bardot and Marilyn Monroe. But my absolute favourite has to be the bright yellow rose named for the beloved cook Julia Child and her obsession with butter.

The symbolic importance of the rose – romantic, religious and political – is just as salient as its botanical significance. The Bronze Age Minoans painted roses on their frescos 3500 years ago. Roses were sacred to the Greek and Roman goddesses of love, Aphrodite and Venus, and one of the many names given to the Virgin Mary is the Mystical Rose.

Strife engulfed England during the War of the Roses, fought between rival branches of the Royal House of Plantagenet in the fifteenth century. The Tudor rose was adopted as a national emblem to represent peace and unity following this long civil war. The rose is the national flower of England and the United States along with eleven other countries.

Arousing and stimulating, the scent of the rose has captured the hearts of humanity like no other flower's scent. I love that the ancient varieties of rose are still the most widely grown for the perfume industry in France, Iran and Turkey. Attar, the highly concentrated oil known also as the soul of the rose, requires a colossal amount of labour to produce. Picked by hand before the sun rises and distilled on the same day, many kilograms of petals are required to make just a few drops of precious oil.

Roses are utterly ubiquitous in our lives. We have filled our gardens, tables, artworks and hearts with blousy blooms, laced candies, cakes and soaps with their scent. But, if we let them, I feel they can remind us that the truly transcendent and the wildly passionate can be found in the everyday.

Aqua flora

The ancient art of distillation involves the use of a still, a heat source, water and a botanical. Distilling creates two fragrant products: essential oil and fragrant water. Fragrant water, called a hydrosol, can also be obtained by using a simple stovetop method that doesn't require a still. The aromatic properties of hydrosols are less concentrated, making them suitable for a variety of perfumery projects, including body and facial sprays, room fresheners, and linen sprays. Rose, jasmine, lavender, citrus blossom, lemon balm, mint, rosemary and rose geranium are just some of the botanicals that are often distilled into hydrosols.

To make a simple hydrosol, place a large saucepan with a lid on a stovetop, and centre an inverted small stainless steel or heatproof glass bowl in the bottom of the pot to create a platform. Place flowers around the bowl, up to the top. Add enough water to cover the blossoms.

Place another stainless steel or heatproof glass bowl on top of the inverted bowl to collect your hydrosol. Make sure there is room between the bowl and the pot's sides to allow steam to rise. Place the lid on the saucepan upside down to enable the steam to condense in the collecting bowl.

Bring the water to a boil and simmer on a medium–low heat to create steam without harming the blossoms. Place as much ice as will fit onto the lid – this will help the steam condense. Replace the ice when it melts.

The process is complete when the blossoms give off no more scent. Remove the pot from the heat and cool to room temperature before removing the lid. Store the hydrosol in a clean, sterile jar. Hydrosols are easily contaminated by poor handling and do not last long. Store them in the refrigerator for up to 2 weeks.

Japanese honeysuckle

LONICERA JAPONICA —————— CAPRIFOLIACEAE

One might imagine that honeysuckles represent what
all nectar tastes like: ambrosia, drink of the gods,
seeping from the core of a blossom. Honeysuckles thrive
throughout summer, attracting bees, butterflies, birds
and children – a bright memory from my childhood
is sucking the sweet liquid from the base of a floret.
The highly familiar Japanese variety grows wild on a
vine with thin, trumpet-like orange and white flowers.
Suffused into a simple syrup, honeysuckles can flavour
a range of summery treats. In the American South,
where the scent of the flower hangs in the humid air,
honeysuckles are whipped into butter and sometimes
adorn hummingbird cake.

Floral vermouth

With roots in Italy, vermouth is essentially a fortified wine with the addition of bitter wormwood *Artemisia absinthium* and other botanicals for flavour. I thought making vermouth was intimidatingly complex alchemy at first, but it turns out it is deceptively simple. It just requires some time and patience. Honeysuckle adds a floral brightness, but I encourage you to experiment with different botanicals and even fruit to create your own unique vermouth that speaks of the season you created it in.

This vermouth has a soft and sweet flavour profile that celebrates the botanicals and produce of spring, forgoing the usual heavy handed spices in a more traditional vermouth. Aim for a vermouth that has 15–18 per cent alcohol by volume (ABV) – a general ratio of 4:1 spirit to wine, depending on the ABV of the spirit you choose. Serve your vermouth with soda water (club soda) for a light, refreshing aperitif, mix it into a martini, or enjoy it straight over ice.

Pack rhubarb, blackberries, lemon peel and raspberry leaf into separate jars to infuse. Cover the botanicals with a neutral high-proof spirit such as vodka. Shake the jars every day for around 2 weeks. Strain out the botanicals.

Pack fennel flowers or pollen, orange blossom, young fig leaves, wormwood, violet blossoms, calendula, camomile and lilac into separate jars to infuse. Cover the botanicals with a neutral, high-proof spirit such as vodka. Shake the jars every day for around 1 week, or until the blossoms and leaves look spent or have lost their colour. Strain out the botanicals.

Combine white wine (traditionally moscato) with equal parts of the infused spirits at a ratio of 4:1. Add a half portion of honeysuckle syrup (follow the recipe for Wisteria syrup on page 69, replacing wisteria with honeysuckle). Taste to see if the flavours are balanced, and add more syrup if necessary. Age your vermouth in a large jar or bottles, adding roasted rhubarb and vanilla pods for a more complex flavour. Age for around 1 week – though practising patience will improve the flavour. Strain the vermouth through muslin (cheesecloth) and bottle it. Store at room temperature but refrigerate once open.

Linden

TILIA X EUROPAEA ——————— MALVACEAE

Known throughout Europe as a lime tree and the United States as a basswood, the linden is easy to recognise once you get to know its romantic, heart-shaped leaves and the slender, leaf-like bracts that cup its discreet flowers. You will likely catch the scent of linden blossoms before you find the tree.

Large, robust and able to thrive for generations, the linden is the tree of lovers in German folklore, associated with Freyja, the Germanic goddess of love, spring and fertility. German villages were once centred on lime trees – they were used as community meeting places, and medieval legal judgments were made *sub tilia*, 'under the lime tree'. Unter den Linden, perhaps the most well-known boulevard in Berlin, means 'under the linden trees'. Lacy linden blossoms envelop the glorious streets of Germany with a thick scent that's an unusual mixture of resiny, floral and herbaceous.

There are many varieties of linden, all edible, and the flowers are best picked soon after they bloom. Tea from the blossoms, known as *tilleul* in France and *lindenbluten* in Germany, is an attempt to replicate this intoxicating scent.

The celebrated French author Marcel Proust plays on these nostalgic associations in *Remembrance of Things Past*. In a famous passage, the narrator dips a madeleine into a honeyed lime-blossom tea and awakens a series of repressed childhood memories. This poetic moment eloquently captures the links between scent, flowers and memory.

Linden madeleines

What better tribute to Proust's narrator than these scallop-shaped cakes, made from a simple mixture and spooned into special moulded baking trays.

To coax out as much linden flavour as possible, infuse and mix the blossoms into as many ingredients as possible – you'll need to pick a generous amount. You can also use these infusing techniques with other edible flowers and for baked treats like shortbread or chiffon cake.

The day before baking your madeleines, infuse about 110–150 g (3¾–5¼ oz/¾–1 cup) plain (all-purpose) flour with linden blossoms (don't forget to remove the blossoms the next day). Next, make the linden sugar. Combine 30 g (1 oz/⅔ cup) linden blossoms with 140 g (5 oz/⅔ cup) sugar. I also infuse about 50 g (1¾ oz/1 cup) linden blossoms directly into 125 ml (4¼ fl oz/½ cup) warm melted butter overnight (re-warm the butter to strain).

Preheat the oven to 190° (375°F). Butter and dust the madeleine pans with flour. With an electric mixer or by hand, whisk 4 eggs, linden sugar and ¼ teaspoon salt together until thick – about 8 minutes. Add 1 teaspoon vanilla extract and 1½ teaspoons freshly grated lemon zest. Using a rubber spatula, fold in the linden flour then the linden butter. Spoon the mixture into your prepared madeleine pans and bake until golden – about 7 minutes. Cool completely, then sprinkle with icing (confectioners') sugar and serve with tea for dipping.

Seville orange

CITRUS AURANTIUM ———— RUTACEAE

Native to India and China, the blossom of the Seville or bitter orange has been thriving for centuries in sun-drenched soils. Evoking purity and beloved by royalty, each waxy flower has five angelic white petals, and the centre is adorned with a set of golden anthers (pollen producers) that sit like a coronet. The craze for orange blossoms spread from Islamic culture to Spain in the ninth century, with the Crusaders introducing the citrus to the rest of the Mediterranean Basin by the eleventh century. While the blossom is not eaten due to its bitter aftertaste, when distilled into floral water or essential oil, bitter orange has long been valued to perfume a wrist, scent a bath and flavour delicacies.

The essential oil, first made by the Tunisians and later introduced to ancient Egypt, was given the name *neroli* in homage to the Italian Princess of Nerola Anne Marie Orsini, who became enamoured with the scent, perfuming her gloves, hair and bathwater with it in the sixteenth century. She is credited with introducing the oil to the Italian upper class and the Sun King, Louis XIV of France. Passionate about perfume from a young age, he suffered from severe headaches, and only the sweet and soothing scent of the orange blossom was said to be bearable for him. The orangery at Versailles is proof of the scent's appeal – a structure made at great expense to house citrus year-round to please the particular palate of a king.

Signifying virtue and everlasting love, orange blossoms have played an important part in the wedding rituals of many cultures, particularly Chinese, where they have been woven into hair, featured in bouquets and embroidered onto dresses. English royal brides have an association with orange blossoms, which began with Queen Victoria marrying Prince Albert in 1840 – instead of a tiara, she wore a simple wreath of orange blossoms.

Alcoholic tincture

You can use tinctures to create fragrant sprays for your body, home or linens, as well as craft traditional perfumes. This uncomplicated method requires little equipment or expertise. It's essential to employ high-proof alcohol – not drinking alcohol like vodka – as it extracts the most fragrance. Avoid using denatured alcohol, rubbing alcohol (isopropyl alcohol) or methanol, as the latter is toxic and easily absorbed through the skin. If you opt for food-grade ethanol, these tinctures can be used to make Floral vermouth (page 55).

To start, fill a sterilised jar with processed blossoms (see pages 42–3), leaving a few centimetres (about an inch) of room at the top. Add alcohol until the flowers are completely submerged, then seal the jar tightly. Store the jar away from sunlight and carefully shake it once a day to ensure all the flower surfaces are coated with alcohol.

Once the petals have lost their colour and form, strain the liquid using a fine-mesh sieve lined with a piece of material. Refresh the alcohol with more petals, repeating the process until the extract's scent meets your preference. You can assess the scent by trying a little on your skin. Fragile flowers like orange blossom, tuberose, lilac and lily of the valley may take as little as 24 hours, while woodier flowers such as lavender can steep for longer.

When the tincture is ready, pour it into a clean container through a paper filter that has been soaked with alcohol, and then store the tincture away from sunlight.

It is a simple process to further concentrate the tincture and make it a longer-lasting perfume. On a warm day leave the tincture outside in an uncovered, shallow dish. There's a chance you may lose some of the light, fresh notes of the perfume during the evaporation process. However, once complete, it will yield a minute quantity of viscous, concentrated oil called an absolute.

Artichoke

CYNARA CARDUNCULUS VAR. *SCOLYMUS* —————— ASTERACEAE

The artichoke has a surprisingly seductive history: it was domesticated from a wild thistle and has been consumed on the shores of the Mediterranean since the time of the ancient Greeks – Homer made mention of its untamed relative, the cardoon, as early as the eighth century BCE.

The edible part of the plant we so enjoy is actually the bud of the artichoke, rarely allowed to flower. The sturdy 'leaves' that are peeled away to expose the soft heart are bracts modified to protect the developing bloom. The unpalatable choke, which we discard, would develop into the vivid purple thistle-like flower head – an inflorescent globe made up of hundreds of tiny, glistening flowers.

To enjoy an artichoke is an act of patience and restraint; the preparation takes time, and not much of the plant remains on the plate. But the tender-hearted artichoke will reward your perseverance. Its very chemical make-up, a compound called cynarine, makes everything eaten afterwards taste all the sweeter. This secret was not lost on aristocratic Europeans – artichokes were in vogue at courts from the mid-seventeenth century, considered a luxurious, vaguely aphrodisiac tidbit.

Incredibly, in the early 1900s the US artichoke market was controlled by the mafia. The so-called artichoke wars lasted years, until the sale, display and possession of artichokes became prohibited in 1935. In 1948 California, young actress Norma Jeane Mortenson, who had only recently taken the stage name Marilyn Monroe, was appointed the state's first honorary Artichoke Queen.

Common Latin terms

Learning about flowers is often also a lesson in Latin. The international binomial system of nomenclature (more on page 24) usually uses a bastardised version of Latin (words are added, grammar changed) that can sound either pleasantly old-fashioned or vexingly pretentious. Here are some common terms to look out for in botanical names that can be helpful in revealing certain characteristics about a plant.

- *africana* – from Africa
- *alata* – winged
- *alba* – white
- *albiflorus* – white-flowered
- *altissima* – tallest
- *amabilis* – lovely
- *aquifolium* – holly-leaved
- *argentea* – silvery
- *australis* – southern
- *canadensis* – from Canada
- *coniferous* – cone-bearing
- *cordate* – heart-shaped
- *densiflorus* – heavily flowered
- *edulis* – edible
- *elegans* – elegant
- *globosa* – globe-shaped
- *gracilis* – graceful
- *grandiflorus* – large-flowered
- *japonica* – from Japan
- *marginatus* – with a stripe
- *nanus* – dwarf
- *nigra* – black
- *officinalis* – medicinal
- *prostratus* – lying flat
- *purpurea* – purple
- *rotundifolius* – round leaves
- *vulgaris* – common

Jack-in-the-pulpit

ARISAEMA TRIPHYLLUM ———————— ARACEAE

**Jack-in-the-pulpit, a unique spring ephemeral, earns
its name from the memorable configuration of its
inflorescence (a beautiful term for the arrangement
of flowers on a stalk). The name certainly captures the
imagination. The flower forms a picture of a preacher –
'Jack' or, more accurately, the spadix – surrounded by
a distinctive chalice-shaped spathe, or modified leaf.
The stunning purple, green and reddish stripes of the
spathe make for a dramatic display in woodlands newly
emerged from winter.**

Native to the eastern United States, Jack-in-the-pulpit is
dioecious, meaning male and female flowers form on separate
plants. The term dioecious derives from the Ancient Greek
dioikía, meaning 'two households'. Many flowering trees,
such as figs, mulberries and gingkoes, are dioecious, while
it is less common in smaller plants. However, what makes
Jack-in-the-pulpit even more intriguing is its ability to change
its sex in response to its circumstances. In a lean year, if the
plant does not have enough sustenance to produce fruit, the
intelligent blossom has evolved to either change back into or
carry on as a male flower. In an abundant year the same plant
might regain confidence and transition into a fertile female
and fruit. An impressive magic trick of evolution and survival.

Floral portraits

The beauty of Jack-in-the-pulpit was not lost on artist Georgia O'Keeffe (1887–1986), who often painted its striped spathe to great effect. Although O'Keeffe, known as the Mother of American Modernism, began her artistic career as a painter of watercolour landscapes, she soon began to use the flowers she had loved since childhood as her subject matter. By the time she was in her mid-thirties, O'Keeffe had developed her signature style in oils – larger-than-life flowers, painted with a vivid beauty that had never been seen before. O'Keeffe's portraits of calla lilies, the related Jack-in-the-pulpit and jimsonweed (a common plant from the poisonous Datura family) are among her most recognised works.

Wisteria

WISTERIA SINENSIS ———————— FABACEAE

Wisteria wraps everything in a haze of fleeting purple abundance, tendrils reaching in all directions. The vine's glorious blossoms dress houses in ephemeral purple robes and perfumed dreams.

Stunningly beautiful, the Asian species was imported to North America and given prominent positions in grand gardens. But they are ropey and wild, spiralling constrictors twining around anything vertical, cutting off the light and air and killing less sturdy species; they grow their own ladders to break into the house. The less flamboyant *Wisteria frutescens*, indigenous to the lower mid-west, south-east and eastern parts of the United States, is more politely mannered. It also blooms on branches that have already grown leaves, unlike its precocious Asian cousin.

Gone in a wink, the blossoms of all wisteria species are edible. Members of the legume family and like the pea flowers they are related to, they are sweetly crisp and delicious. All other parts of the plant – stems, leaves, pods, anything green – are toxic and must be avoided at all costs. Rise early and collect your blossoms first thing in the morning when their scent is at its peak, and use the open, fragrant flowers for syrup or vinegar.

Wisteria syrup

The dainty perfume of spring is captured in this floral syrup. Wisteria has a delicate scent that is damaged by heat, so a cold infusion is used here. Open blossoms will impart the most flavour, so remove those from the stalks. Take care to avoid any leaves or stalks, which are toxic.

Bring 220 g (7¾ oz/1 cup) sugar and 250 ml (8½ fl oz/1 cup) water to a gentle boil on the stove. Stir to ensure all the sugar dissolves, then take the mixture off the heat and cool to room temperature. Gently place about 100 g (3½ oz/2 cups) open wisteria blossoms in a sterilised jar, then pour in the cooled sugar liquid, leaving a few centimetres (about an inch) of room at the top of the jar. Steep the mixture for 24 hours before straining out the blossoms using a fine-mesh sieve.

Wisteria syrup stores well in the fridge. Use it to add a light floral touch to cocktails, drizzle it over ice cream or whip it into cream for a spring pavlova.

Other flowers that make beautiful syrups are honeysuckle, elderflower, magnolia, violet and lilac.

Black locust

ROBINIA PSEUDOACACIA ———— FABACEAE

**When the fleeting and generous blossoms of the black locust
appear in late spring, I recommend you drop any other activity
and swiftly attend their short season of one to two weeks.
Sprays of ivory blossoms hang from branches like plump
icicles and diffuse a languid, vanilla-like perfume into the
air. Native to the United States, these trees are a common
sight on many urban streetscapes, popular for that beautiful
scent and their hardiness. Introduced to Europe in the early
seventeenth century, and known there as acacia or robinia,
they have become a beloved part of the landscape and cuisine.**

Only the pea-like blossoms are edible – all other parts of the tree
are toxic. Best plucked when just unfurling, the blossoms can be
infused cold into syrup (page 69) or fermented into a floral soda
(page 96). They also have a beautiful silky texture when eaten raw
and surrender in your mouth with a lovely sweetness.

Black locust beignets

Known as *fiori di acacia fritti* in Italy, these exceptional fritters are often made
with beer batter. I prefer to replace the beer with Wild fermented soda (page 96)
or kombucha (page 163) as it supports the perfume of the blossoms.

In a bowl combine 100 g (3 oz/^{2}/$_3$ cup) plain (all-purpose) flour, ½ teaspoon salt and
1 tablespoon sugar. Stir well to combine. Whisk in 160 ml (5½ fl oz/^{2}/$_3$ cup) cold soda
or kombucha. Let the mixture rest in the fridge for 30 minutes.

Heat 150 ml (5 fl oz /^{2}/$_3$ cup) olive oil over medium–high heat in a pan. Test with a drop
of batter – if it floats and sizzles at once the oil is hot enough. Separately dip 20 black
locust flower clusters into the batter. Shake off the excess – you only want a light
amount of batter. Lay each cluster in the hot oil, frying 5–6 at a time. Turn after a
minute; each side should be dark golden. Lay on kitchen paper to absorb the extra oil,
then dust with icing (confectioners') sugar to serve.

Paulownia

PAULOWNIA TOMENTOSA —————— PAULOWNIACEAE

In Japan, there is a wonderful tradition of planting paulownia – or empress trees – to honour the birth of a baby girl. It was said they would mature by the time the girl was ready to marry and could be sold for her dowry – wishes for the baby to develop strong, beautiful and resilient like a paulownia, planted into reality. The tree is named for the regal beauty Russian princess Anna Pavlovna, granddaughter of Catherine the Great.

Native to China and valued for their meteoric growth, strong wood, and benefits for soil regeneration and air purification, paulownia can grow up to 6 metres (20 ft) in the first year. The valuable wood made a target for brazen thieves and in the 1980s a spate of crimes against mature trees occurred, with rustlers cutting down public trees to sell the wood in Japan to be used for bridal trousseau chests, jewellery boxes and coffins. Luckily paulownia has a phoenix-like ability to renew itself once cut down, although its rapid growth and ability to reproduce has landed it on many invasive species lists.

Paulownia's foxglove-like blossoms frost each branch in generous panicles, a booming symphony that is hard to ignore. The edible blossoms are nectar rich and more heavily doused in sweet vanilla perfume than a Chanel beauty counter.

Floral pilgrimages

In North America, paulownia were planted broadly as an ornamental tree, lining prominent streets in many major cities, including in industrial landscapes. While there is something magical about finding a beautiful flower on a city corner, there is also something incredible about crossing the world for a bloom. Here are some garden pilgrimages I would recommend.

- Wave Hill, New York, United States
- Conservatory Garden in Central Park, New York, United States
- Planting Fields Arboretum, Long Island, New York, United States
- Longwood Gardens in Kennett Square, Pennsylvania, United States
- Jardín Botánico de Vallarta, Puerto Vallarta, Mexico
- Château de Villandry, Villandry, France
- Claude Monet's garden, Giverny, France
- Oudolf Field at Hauser & Wirth, Somerset, United Kingdom
- Sissinghurst Castle Garden, Kent, United Kingdom
- Keukenhof, Lisse, Netherlands
- Le Jardin Majorelle, Marrakech, Morocco
- Garden of Ninfa, Cisterna di Latina, Italy
- Kyoto Botanical Gardens, Kyoto, Japan

Grape hyacinth

MUSCARI ARMENIACUM ———— ASPARAGACEAE

The grape hyacinth creates an effortless stroke of vibrant blue in a spring garden. Tiny stems produce spirals of globular flowers that open to an urn shape in the same colour as bluebells and common hyacinths, to which they're related. Interestingly they are also in the same plant family as asparagus and agave. The name *Muscari* derives from the Greek word for musk, *moschos*, and refers to the scent of some species, most of which are native to the Mediterranean and Central Asia.

The Dutch, undisputed masters of a primavera bulb display, use flowerbeds like a canvas, expertly composing colour on the earth. The Keukenhof gardens at Lisse in the Netherlands – the famous 'garden of Europe' where seven million bulbs are planted annually – contain an area of grape hyacinth known as the Blue River.

Like many plants, *Muscari* are a pH indicator; they contain anthocyanin, which changes the vivid blue pigment of their petals to a pinkish red with the addition of acid. While hyacinths are toxic, the grape-flavoured flowers of grape hyacinths are not, and a syrup can create a colour-changing beverage with a simple squeeze of lemon. Lemonade stand or magic show? Violets and blue butterfly peas are among many other plants with this mystical secret.

Layering bulbs

When I lived in New York I was astounded
by the beauty of a small front garden
I often passed; the very modest bed was
in constant bloom with successive spring
bulbs. How on earth did they all fit in?
I have since learned of a technique the
Dutch call a bulb lasagne – a clever layering
of bulbs that achieves successive flowering
in small beds or pots.

The idea is to fill your pots with different
types of bulbs, potting the largest and
latest-flowering ones first, working
upwards and finishing off with the
smallest and earliest-flowering ones
at the top of the pot. When the lower
layer bulbs start to shoot, they
manoeuvre around anything they
meet above and carry on growing.
For example, you might put
lace tulips or snowdrops in the
lower layer, grape hyacinths
or daffodils in the middle,
then crocuses or fritillaries
on top for an extended
display of colour.

Poppy

PAPAVER SOMNIFERUM ——————— PAPAVERACEAE

From Himalayan blue to yellow Arctic, orange Moroccan to white oriental, the lilac poppy of Troy to red corn, this varied group of opportunistic annuals is as colourful as it is widespread – vivid petals that dance with the wind like a crumpled chiffon skirt. There are hundreds of poppy species across the world, mostly in the northern hemisphere, and possibly just as many traditional uses.

Papaver is Latin for 'food' or 'milk', and the seeds of common red poppies have likely germinated alongside cornfields for as long as humans have cultivated crops. Poppyseed cake, made from a paste of seeds and sugar, is traditional in Central Europe, and the seeds are also used to decorate and add a nutty flavour to breads and pastries. The oil is used for cooking, and to make paint, varnish and soap. A red dye can be obtained from corn poppy petals, which can also be made into ink.

Use of the famous opium poppy dates back to at least the Bronze Age Minoans, and possibly to the Neolithic era (5000 BCE). Its properties as a sedative and painkiller have made it valuable in modern medicine, known through time for its treatment of anxiety and pain, but also for its dangers – the poppy is a symbol of Morpheus, the Greek god of dreams, but was also dedicated to Hypnos and Thanatos, the gods of sleep and death. During the nineteenth century, opium use in Europe and North America was widespread and socially acceptable, with opulent dens catering to artists, literary figures and politicians alike. Art and opium have long been linked, with poets such as Lord Byron and painters including Picasso seeking the oblivion of the drug.

Most poppies are useful for attracting beneficial insects to a garden. It is thought the black marks found on the inside petals of some poppy species mimic a female beetle, luring in pollinating males.

Floral anatomy

The marks on the poppy's petals speak to a complex floral reproductive anatomy. Understanding the common parts of a flower will help you to observe any bloom more closely.

The sepal (1) is the modified leaf beneath the flower. It protects the flower in budding.

The stamen includes all male parts of the flower:

- The anther (2) is the male reproductive cell. It contains pollen.
- The filament (3) supports the anther.

The pistil includes all female parts of the flower:

- The ovary (4) is the flower's female reproductive organ.
- The stigma (5) is the structure atop the ovary that receives pollen.
- The style (6) is the stalk that connects the stigma and ovary.
- The ovule (7) is the reproductive cell. It forms a seed when fertilised with pollen.

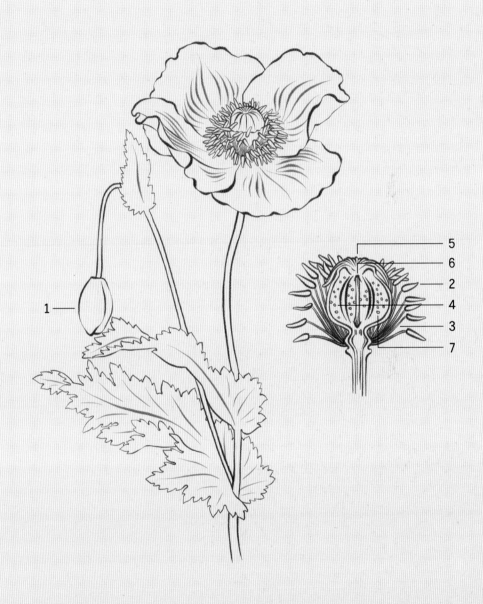

Gladiolus

GLADIOLUS NANUS ——————— IRIDACEAE

Native to Africa, Europe and Central Asia, these members of the iris family are a contradiction of luxurious jewel-hued edible petals and hardy root stock. 'Gladdies' once felt like a gaudy pastiche flower, favourite of the gloriously outrageous Dame Edna Everage – brash, loud, not to be taken seriously. But the more dainty and modest wild forms call to my heart, at home among the wheat fields of Italy and Iran, displaying a humble few slimmer-petalled flowers, rather than dozens of enormous lurid spikes.

The scientific name translates as 'little sword' from the Latin, due to the spear shape of the leaves, and was coined by Roman naturalist Pliny the Elder in the first century. Legend tells that gladiolus blooms were thrown to Roman gladiators after battle in honour of their victory.

While gladiolus flowers are edible, parts of the plant are toxic to eat and the sap can irritate the skin. Despite this, in many parts of Africa the corms are used in a range of traditional medicines. An infusion of petals warmed by the sun is used as a soothing wash for tired feet.

Petal plates

Gladiolus flowers taste slightly tart and vegetal, so they are best used as jewel-hued containers for seafood or salad. Pick blooms in the morning before the sun dries them. Wash the flowers gently, pat them dry and place them in a moistened plastic bag with a little air space left in it. Put the bag into the fridge. Take the flowers out of the fridge a few minutes before serving, and dip them into ice-cold water to freshen them. Remove the stamens before filling the flowers.

Pink lady's slipper

CYPRIPEDIUM ACAULE ———— ORCHIDACEAE

The prehistoric Orchidaceae family boasts a staggering 25,000 members and is second in size only to the very prolific Asteraceae. It continues to grow almost daily, with intrepid botanists still stumbling upon unrecorded varieties in far-flung corners of the globe. Orchids are beloved for their flamboyant and exotic blooms, which are vibrant and varied in colour, form and size. According to Guinness World Records, the world's most minute orchid, *Platystele jungermannioides,* is found in the lower cloud forest of Mexico, Guatemala, Costa Rica and Panama, and grows to mere 6 mm (0.25 in) high.

Orchid blooms follow the standard structure of monocots (grass-like flowering plants), with their floral components – stamen, petals and sepals – appearing in multiples of three. On a slipper orchid, one of the petals, called the lip or labellum, is grotesquely distorted in shape and size, and forms a pouch that makes one think of a slipper or shoe. The distinctive and striking pink lip of the pink lady's slipper is the outcome of the orchid's coevolution with insects.

Bees are necessary for the pollination of pink lady's slipper. Lured into the pouch by its vibrant colour and deceptively sweet scent, the bee finds no nectar within and attempts to leave. Curling inward at the edges, the lip traps the bee and prevents it from returning the way it entered. Inside the pouch, hairs and light lead the bee on to a pair of openings at the top, one beneath each pollen deposit. To escape, the bee must be exposed to the flower's reproductive organs. It is a complicated procreation pattern, and not a particularly fruitful one.

Orchid fever

Orchid fever refers to the intense passion that people have for rare and exotic orchids. This phenomenon has led many individuals to go to extreme lengths to hunt for such orchids, often risking their lives and breaking the law in the process.

The quest for rare orchids dates back to the Victorian era, when orchid hunting became a popular hobby among the upper class. While today's collectors still go to great lengths to hunt for these rare blooms, many orchids are now protected by international law, with severe penalties for rulebreakers. In recent years, the internet has made it easier to find rare orchids, and some specimens have sold for hundreds of thousands of dollars.

One rare and valuable orchid is *Nymphaea thermarum*, also known as the world's smallest water lily, which was discovered in Rwanda in 1987. This tiny plant is critically endangered, with only a handful of specimens remaining in the wild. In 2014, one of the last remaining *Nymphaea thermarum* plants was stolen from Kew Gardens in London in the United Kingdom. This was believed to be the work of a professional thief targeting the plant, which was estimated to be worth over £20,000 on the black market. The theft sparked outrage and prompted Kew Gardens to increase security measures around their valuable plant collections.

Orchid fever is a phenomenon that has existed for centuries, driving people to hunt for the rare and exotic plants at great personal risk. While some orchid hunters have used illegal and unethical methods to obtain their prizes, others have contributed to the scientific understanding of orchids and helped to expand their availability to the general public. Despite the dangers and legal implications, the allure of rare orchids continues to captivate collectors and enthusiasts around the world.

Gardenia

GARDENIA JASMINOIDES ———————— RUBIACEAE

White gardenia flowers have always had an aura of luxury, perhaps because they were formerly imported to Europe and North America from warmer climes, and grown at great expense under glass. In her novel *The Age of Innocence*, Edith Wharton wrote of New York City's upper-class men sporting these flowers in their buttonholes around the late 1800s. The popular garden plant *Gardenia jasminoides* is one of more than one hundred gardenias found in the tropics from which its relative the coffee plant also hails. Most bear similar white, fragrant flowers that seem to unwind as they open, oozing a sensuous perfume.

The delicate flowers, set off by dark green glossy foliage, have inspired Chinese art for more than 1000 years and have been grown in Chinese gardens since before 1000 BCE. The flower's scent is often described as 'intoxicating' or 'sultry', so it's no surprise that it's promoted as a sexual stimulant and is used in perfumes, lotions and candles. The flowers can also be eaten: buds can be pickled or preserved in honey, the petals crystallised, or the flowers used to make tea, similar in taste to jasmine tea.

Flowers for a sensual night garden

The scent of gardenias is usually at its peak after dark. Here are some other flowers to plant if you'd like to enjoy a heavenly perfumed stroll around your garden in the evening.

- star jasmine – an evergreen climbing shrub with clusters of white flowers and an irresistible perfume
- moonflower – this vine's trumpet-shaped fragrant flowers open at dusk and close in the morning
- night-scented phlox – tiny white flowers curl up in the day but open their star-shaped petals at night
- queen of the night – a species of cactus that blooms only at night; its flowers wilt before dawn
- sacred datura – a night-blooming herbaceous perennial, related to tomatoes, eggplants and potatoes
- night-scented tobacco plant – a jasmine-like fragrance emerges from the trumpet-shaped blossoms when they open at night

Phlox

PHLOX PANICULATA —————— POLEMONIACEAE

Found mostly in North America (there's one lonely species in Siberia), phlox was one of the first wildflowers from the 'New World' to be collected by explorers and taken back to Europe. There, it became a popular garden plant due to its no-fuss nature and long flowering season.

The clouds of billowy phlox blooms come in nearly every hue, but the word phlox comes from the Greek for 'fire' or 'flame', referring to the intense pinks and reds of common species. The flowers are edible and taste spicy-sweet; however, the flowers of creeping phlox (*Phlox subulata*) are less digestible and should be avoided.

Wild blue phlox (*Phlox divaricata*) and Rocky Mountain phlox (*Phlox multiflora*) are still valued for their medicinal properties by First Nations people in North America, although this specialised knowledge is traditionally only shared with those who have a right to use the plants. The Cheyenne reportedly once used the leaves to treat body numbness, and the leaves and flowers were pounded to make a stimulating body wash.

Beautiful botanical terms

- calyx – the outer part of a flower, usually a whorl of sepals, that protects the petals as they form a bud
- cauliflory – refers to a plant or tree that flowers directly from the main stem or trunk, such as the redbud; a common trait in tropical regions, as seen on the papaya tree, cacao tree and coffee plant
- dioecious – when male and female flowers form on individual plants, for example gingko or asparagus; monoecious plants grow male and female flowers on the same plant
- floret – one small flower that is part of a composite flower head
- inflorescence – a group or cluster of flowers arranged on a stem; types include catkin (a downy, hanging spike, usually without petals, on trees such as willow and hazel), raceme (a simple floral spike with flowers growing on short stalks of equal length, such as lily of the valley), umbel (a cluster of flowers with stalks of equal length that grow from one central axis, such as Queen Anne's lace), and spadix (minute flowers covering a fleshy axis, typically protected by a spathe or large leaf-like bract, common to the Arum family, including Jack-in-the-pulpit)
- labellum – a central petal at the base of an orchid flower, larger in size than the other petals and typically different in appearance
- pedicel – a small stalk holding the individual floret of an inflorescence
- plicate – folded like a fan
- pruinose – dusted with white, powdery granules that give a frosted appearance
- rosette – a circular arrangement of leaves at the base of a flower stem

Elderflower

SAMBUCUS NIGRA ———————— ADOXACEAE

The sumptuous panicles of elderflower, generous, lace-like and elegant, frost the shrub in a cream mist from mid-spring to late summer, followed by succulent blue-black fruit. I love the joyous depiction of elderflower in David Hockney's painting *Elderflower Blossom, Kilham, July 2006*, which shows an East Yorkshire hedgerow full of elderflower seemingly at the peak of its short season, blazing in the bright sun of a summer day. You can almost smell the attractive lemony scent through the canvas.

In Greek mythology, Prometheus is said to have carried hot coals in the stem of an elderflower plant when he stole fire from the gods on Mount Olympus, and elder gets its name from the Anglo-Saxon word for fire, *aeld*. The genus name, *Sambucus,* refers to an ancient wind instrument called a sambuca, made from hollowed-out twigs or stems.

During the Middle Ages, folklore held that it was good fortune if elder planted herself in your backyard; it meant that the 'Mother' had chosen to protect your house, family and animals against witchcraft and unnamed terrors. It also meant you should pay respects to the elder, never cutting or burning it without praying to the Mother first. 'The Elder-Tree Mother', an 1845 fairytale by Hans Christian Andersen, tells the story of a little boy who, while sick in bed, is given elderflower tea by his mother and soon sees visions, beginning with an elderberry tree growing from the teapot.

A gentle distillation of elderflowers produces a sweet and heady water, while a cold infusion, made by leaving the flowers to steep in water overnight, is equally lovely. To harvest these alluring flowers, pollinators provide the best guide: on a dry day, the more insects on the panicles, the nearer the peak of perfection they are. The green parts of elderflower are considered toxic, but the uses for this edible flower and its ripe berries, which should only be consumed after cooking, are infinite and thrilling.

Wild fermented soda

Make a wild fermented elderflower soda to catch and keep the ephemeral late-spring scent of the blossom. It makes exquisite frozen popsicles, long drinks and cocktails, and can be used in baking, salad dressings and fruity desserts – think elderflower-infused strawberries. Elderflower can also be fermented further into a beautiful vinegar – simply let the soda ferment a bit longer to become more alcoholic, and then follow part two of the process for making Lilac vinegar on page 35.

In a large pot, bring 3.8 litres (1 gallon) distilled or spring water to the boil (the chlorine in tap water will harm the yeast). Add 440 g sugar (15½ oz/2 cups) or 350 g honey (12¼ oz/2 cups), and the juice and peel of 3 lemons. Stir well until the sugar (or honey) has dissolved. Take the mixture off the heat and cool to room temperature.

Collect around 100–200 g (3½–7 oz/2–4 cups) elderflower (or other seasonal aromatic) blossoms. Remove all the petite flowers from the stalks. Avoid washing the flowers to retain the wild yeast for the fermentation process.

Add the flowers to a sterilised large, open-mouthed jar, and carefully pour in the cooled liquid, leaving at least a few centimetres (an inch) of room at the top of the jar. Cover the jar with a cloth or an airlock to allow air flow. (You want to discourage pests while still allowing the fermentation gasses to escape.) The rate of fermentation will depend on the concentration of yeast and the temperature. Bubbles generally start to rise 3–5 days into the fermentation process. Within another 2 days, the elderflowers will start to rise up out of the jar. At this stage, strain out the flowers using a fine-mesh sieve and bottle the soda. Leave the bottles at room temperature for another day to allow fermentation to continue and create a nice amount of carbonation. Then refrigerate your soda and enjoy within a week or so!

Cardamom

ELETTARIA CARDAMOMUM ———————— ZINGIBERACEAE

**Cardamom is known as the queen of spices. But, if you
are buying or foraging for a cardamom plant, make
sure you have the true or green cardamom (*Elettaria
cardamomum*) and not false cardamom (*Alpinia nutans*);
its white flowers are marked with yellow, not pink.
The flowers of true cardamom are tiny, and produced
in spikes at the base of the plant.**

Elettaria cardamomum grows in the subtropical hills of
south-west India but its fragrant seeds are so adaptable
that it is now used throughout the world in sweet or savoury
dishes. Its warming taste is a key ingredient in spicy chai,
and in wintery European dishes such as rice pudding, mulled
wine and Christmas baking. Its better-tasting cousin, black
or greater cardamom (*Amomum subulatum*), has black seeds
that are used in cooking in India and South-East Asia.

Cardamom has been used in medicine since at least the fourth
century BCE. Ancient Greek physician Hippocrates wrote
about its medicinal properties and benefits after a heavy meal,
and in many cultures whole seed pods are chewed after a
meal to aid digestion and sweeten breath.

Paper incense

When making incense papers, your goal is to overcome the smell of the burning paper, so heavy fragrances should be used – think rose, lemon myrtle or cardamom.

Cut white blotter paper – into flower shapes, of course! Stir 1 teaspoon potassium nitrate (you can buy potassium nitrate over the counter at most chemist drug stores) into 125 ml (4¼ fl oz/½ cup) warm water until completely dissolved. Soak the paper flowers in the solution until thoroughly wet, then hang them up to dry.

Choose a tincture (see instructions on making tinctures on page 60) and add a few drops at a time to the paper. Smear over one side, hang to dry again, then store in an airtight container until ready to use.

To use, simply light one end of your dried paper. When it has a good flame going, quickly blow it out and put it on a fireproof dish to smoulder.

Garden pansy

VIOLA × WITTROCKIANA ———————— VIOLACEAE

Wild pansies (*Viola tricolor*) have a long history of use in herbalism and folk medicine, and are associated with several Roman and Greek myths based on love and jealousy. In Shakespeare's *Hamlet*, Ophelia says, 'There is pansies; that's for thoughts,' perhaps referring to the etymology of pansy, which comes from the French word *pensiez* meaning remembrance or thought. Thus when a bouquet is given to you it sweetly means 'I am thinking of you'. The pansy features heavily in folklore – if you spot one in your dreams, it may signify a falling out with a good friend in your future.

The much larger garden pansies, with their flamboyant 'faces', were bred from the wild pansy in the 1800s, and now come in just about any colour you can dream of. Like other violas, they have edible flowers and leaves.

Pressing flowers

Pressing flowers is a lovely way to preserve the ephemeral beauty of your favourite blooms. It is a simpler alternative to drawing that even beginners can use to create a record of the seasons.

Select fresh flowers in full bloom and free of blemishes. Thin, delicate flowers like pansies and forget-me-nots are ideal for pressing. Remove excess leaves and thick stems, and wipe away any dirt or moisture with a soft cloth.

There are several ways to press flowers, including using a flower press, a heavy book or an iron. The most common method is to use a flower press, which can be made at home using cardboard and paper, or purchased from most craft stores. Etsy has a beautiful selection of ornate handmade presses.

Once you have selected your pressing method, lay your flowers out on a sheet of acid-free paper or cardboard, ensuring they don't touch each other. Place another sheet of paper or cardboard on top of them, and then put the entire stack between the pages of a heavy book or into your flower press – if using an iron, opt for a sheet of paper and gently press the iron over it for a few seconds, then place the flowers into a press or heavy book.

Leave your flowers in the press or book for several days to weeks, depending on their thickness. Check on them occasionally, and replace the paper if it becomes damp. Once your flowers are fully pressed and dry, carefully remove them from the paper or cardboard. You can use them for a variety of crafts or to decorate a cake!

Remember, the key to pressing flowers is to be patient and gentle. With a little time and effort, you can create beautiful pressed-flower creations that will last for years to come.

Blue butterfly pea

CLITORIA TERNATEA ———————— FABACEAE

The colourful blue butterfly pea plant has fascinated humans for centuries. In India it has long been revered as a holy flower and used in daily religious puja offerings. Today, scientists are excited by its ability to produce a plant protein that has potential medical and agricultural uses.

This perennial, fast-growing vine is native to Africa and tropical Asia, and the bright blue of the flowers is nearly as eye-catching as their shape, which resembles female genitalia. Probably for this reason, in Chinese medicine it is believed to affect the female libido. In Ayurvedic medicine it is credited with having antidepressant, sedative and memory-enhancing properties. It has been traditionally used in Thailand and Vietnam to make a relaxing tea.

The plant's spectacular colour-changing property has won it new fans in more recent times. The flower creates a blue drink, which changes colour to purple-pink when acidic lemon is added; a number of gin manufacturers now use the dye in their product after it was discovered that adding tonic water has the same effect, making for 'magical' cocktails. The food dye is also used to colour desserts and rice dishes in South-East Asia. Butterfly pea flower tea is a naturally occurring 'pH indicator', changing colour according to the pH of other ingredients – not unlike the way hydrangeas bloom blue in acidic soils, pink in alkaline soils, and purple when the soil is somewhere in the middle.

Magical cocktail

Butterfly pea flowers put the spotlight on the way science can sometimes seem like magic! When acid (like lemon juice) is added, the vibrant blue of the butterfly pea flower changes to purple, then pink. Furthermore, their understated taste makes them highly versatile, as they won't disrupt the flavour profile of other ingredients.

Try this floral bouquet in a glass for a fragrant twist on a gin sour cocktail.

Start by making a blue butterfly pea simple syrup. Combine 1 part boiling water, 1 part sugar and 1 part dried blue butterfly pea flowers. Stir until the sugar dissolves, then allow the syrup to cool.

In a cocktail shaker, add 45 ml (1½ fl oz) gin, 10 ml (⅓ fl oz) Lillet Blanc, 15 ml (½ fl oz) Wild fermented soda (see page 96), 15 ml (½ fl oz) blue butterfly pea simple syrup, 15 ml (½ fl oz) homemade floral syrup (see Wisteria syrup, page 69), 30 ml (1 fl oz) lemon juice, and 1 egg white. Add ice and shake to combine.

Strain the cocktail into a glass and garnish with a few drops of bitters and fresh flowers.

Pineapple weed

MATRICARIA DISCOIDEA —————— ASTERACEAE

Pineapple weed can be used in place of its cousin chamomile, and exudes a delicious aroma of pineapple and apple when crushed, transporting you to tropical paradise. Most likely the common name refers to the plant's fruity scent, but the small yellowish-green orb flowers also look a bit like tiny pineapples. Up close they resemble the centres of daisies with the ray-like petals plucked off. Indeed, pineapple weed's Latin name refers to this trait – *discoidea* means 'without rays'. Greenish flowers are not that common outside the grass family (Poaceae) – another reason this plant is so special.

Pineapple weed is native to North America, where the First Peoples treasured the plant's scent: it was used to line bedding and cradles, and children wore necklaces of the buds to help repel insects. Pineapple weed can be steeped to make a tea or fermented with sugar and water (and maybe pineapple rind) to produce a fizzy drink not unlike Mexican tepache. Look for this tough little plant with low clumps of feathery, finely dissected leaves growing along roadsides and on gravelly paths in full sun.

Pineapple weed shortbread

This simple recipe highlights the flavour of pineapple weed flowers and lets them shine.

Rub 3 tablespoons pineapple weed flower heads and the zest of 1 lemon into 115 g (4 oz/½ cup) caster (superfine) sugar with your fingers to release the oils from the botanicals into the sugar.

Cream 250 g (9 oz/1 cup) softened butter until light and fluffy, then add 80 g (3 oz/⅓ cup) of the sugar mix along with ½ teaspoon salt, and mix until combined. Add 260 g (9 oz/1¾ cups) plain (all-purpose) flour to the mixture and stir until just combined. Roll out the dough between 2 sheets of baking paper, then chill until firm – about 20 minutes – and cut into desired shapes. Chill again, for at least 10 minutes, and preheat the oven to 160° (320°F). Bake until firm but not yet browning, about 12 minutes, and allow to cool for 10 minutes or so before sprinkling over the remaining sugar mix.

Water lily

NYMPHAEA VIOLACEA ——————— NYMPHAEACEAE

Water lilies were one of the earliest flowering plants to evolve, and humans have admired them for millennia. Both the ancient Egyptian and Mayan cultures considered them sacred, with garlands scattered around the coffin of Egyptian pharaoh Ramesses II, and buds and flowers featuring regularly in Mayan art. It is likely both cultures used the plant as a food source, a medicine, and for ceremonies, especially those linked to death, rebirth and the afterlife. A tea made from the buds is said to have psychoactive effects and it's thought that both the Egyptians and Mayans used it to produce a state of shamanic ecstasy.

Nymphaea flowers, fruits, seeds and rhizomes are considered edible, raw or cooked; cooking reduces the bitterness of particular species. Many different plants are described by the common name 'water lily' and some are more edible than others. In Europe and North America, the yellow water lily (*Nuphar* spp.), which has far smaller petals, sits within the same family as *Nymphaea* but its rhizomes contain tannins and alkaloids that mean it needs far more preparation to make it edible.

Lotus seeds and roots are eaten in many cultures, but these plants are from the unrelated genus *Nelumbo*. Both water lilies and lotuses are inextricably linked in my mind to the Vietnamese Zen Buddhist spiritual leader Thich Nhat Hanh, who wrote *No Mud, No Lotus: The Art of Transforming Suffering,* which reminds us that without the suffering of the mud, we cannot find the blossoming joy of the lotus. Just one of the infinite pearls of wisdom to be gained from the close observation of flowers.

Monet's water lilies

During his lifetime, French artist Claude Monet (1840–1926) painted more than 250 water lily paintings. 'These landscapes of water and reflection have become an obsession,' he wrote in 1908. Monet planted water lilies in his colourful garden at Giverny, which he considered his 'finest masterpiece'. His water lily paintings, with their focus on vivid colour and expressive brushwork, are examples of the early abstract art that placed Monet at the forefront of the impressionist movement. The Musée de l'Orangerie in the beautiful Tuileries Garden in Paris famously houses eight of Monet's immersive water lily murals, arranged in two oval rooms to form an infinity symbol.

Peony

PAEONIA OFFICINALIS —————— PAEONIACEAE

The *Paeonia* genus is the only one in its plant family, and grows naturally on rocky hillsides in Asia, Europe and North America. The blousy-looking lush blooms close overnight or when it's cloudy, making them seem even more beautiful when the sun shines and they open. Sumptuous and subtle at the same time, they last but a few days in a vase – shifts in the shade of the petals tracking their ageing – before they dramatically shatter, throwing their petals over every possible surface and revealing the often contrasting colours of their hearts.

There are a few different stories about how the peony got its name. In one from Greek mythology, Paean, physician of the gods, used a peony to treat a wound for Zeus. Paean's teacher, Asclepius, the god of medicine, flew into a jealous rage, and Zeus saved Paean's life by transforming him into a peony flower. The peony is one of the oldest-referenced flowers in the East; the large, elegant flowers, traditionally referred to as 'king of the flowers', are used symbolically in Chinese art. The peony is also an important bloom in Serbian folklore: *Paeonia peregrina*, known as the Kosovo peony, symbolises the blood of Serbian warriors who lost their lives in the Battle of Kosovo.

Most peonies are small, herbaceous perennials, but in Tibet and central China some form tall woody shrubs called tree peonies. A huge range of flower shapes and colours has been developed by breeders around the world. The flowers are globular and heavy in the hand as a ball of silk, with flower types named dramatically for the complex, sculptural forms they take: anemone, an other-worldly sea creature transported to dry land; bomb, an explosion of innumerable vibrant petals.

Some peonies are edible but not all, so it's important to be sure which type you have; all parts of *Paeonia officinalis* are poisonous, for example. In China, the petals of certain peonies are parboiled and sweetened as a tea. An infusion of peony petals was enjoyed as a refreshing drink in the Middle Ages. The fragrant, pretty petals of edible species can be added to salads and used to decorate drinks, and are perfect for body products.

How to draw a flower

I draw what I see: the whole, solid shapes and larger forms first, then petals, stems and, as the details become smaller and more refined, the stamens and pistils. I fill in the gaps with objects hiding inside the whole.

I vary line weight to suggest shape and form. To me, a consistent line does not convey the life and movement of a plant. It does not convey the hand of the artist. A drawing always begins with a simple line to work out composition, form and shape on the page: how negative space and form dance with each other, pushing and pulling each other's energy. A good line will feel graceful and fluid. It will come straight from experience, those uncountable hours of looking, all unconscious muscle memory, habit, instinct and a mind calmed by the act of simply holding a pen. I can do this because I have done it 10,000 times before, for innumerable days. It is a moving meditation of grace and ease. My right hand – my drawing hand – takes over and my mind is still. This is the closest I come to the divine: the stillness and presence it takes to make one single mark and then another and then another.

Tiny marks multiply and fill up the page. The flower takes shape. My gaze moves back and forth between drawing and reference the whole time. Assessing. Is this angle correct? Does this line weight capture the delicacy of form? Can the drawn petals dance with the wind like their real-life counterparts? I am drawing the one peony I see, but I am also drawing every other peony I have ever seen before it. My internal catalogue – those 10,000 hours of looking – fires up to help me get it right, to capture the essence of this one peony. And you can see it in the work, the progression. Each peony better than the one before it. Sure, my hand improves, lines become smoother and more fluid, but the eye does, too. All that time spent looking and taking mental notes – this is how the leaf notch of an anemone differs from that of a poppy, and this is how they are the same.

I find connection points and minute detail are really important to capture the essence of a flower. I consider the point where a leaf connects to a stem, or a tepal to a bud. These terminals can often be overlooked in our haste to capture a showy petal or patterned leaf. In my early work, I would avoid including them, instead filling the page with one blossom overlapped by another showy blossom. Now I find these in-between moments, these small details, are the heart of the work. The glue that binds it all together and gives it authenticity are the bits that took me years to notice and appreciate – the quiet, the humble and the seemingly insignificant. There is much to be learned in the appreciation of the mundane. I have found a deep, abiding love for a leaf notch that cannot be taken away from me. I can find this love everywhere something grows. It is an ordinary, everyday blessing.

Drawing flowers is seeing and celebrating both repetition and divergence. The peony in front of me is just like every other peony in most ways, yet it will not be identical to any other peony in the history of the earth. How do I capture that? What information do I include and what can I leave out? The infinite variations are exciting! I draw on every peony I've seen and delighted in before this one. I commit them to a page because I love them, because they will die and I want to remember their beauty. I want to remember how they made me feel, how they busied my hand, slowed my mind and stopped my heart.

Dandelion

TARAXACUM OFFICINALE ———————— ASTERACEAE

The humble dandelion, like many of its prolific cousins from the daisy or Asteraceae family – the largest plant family on earth with some 24,000 species – is quite simply ingenious when it comes to the matter of propagation and survival. It is often seen as a trespasser assailing the peace of many a suburban lawn owner, something that must be sprayed out of existence. But its joyous yellow face and tenacious roots have sustained humans for millennia, so perhaps we should take a moment to consider its resourcefulness and beauty. Some of the most surprising discoveries come from the world of the familiar.

Seduced by the sun, a dandelion opens its flower head in the morning and closes it sleepily at night. Known for its bitter leaves – thought to be the herbs present at the last supper – all parts of the plant are edible and wonderfully nourishing.

A dandelion flower head is another inflorescence, in this case a compound inflorescence, containing 100 to 300 ray flowers or florets densely packed together, giving the impression of a single puffball. Each ray flower has a strap-shaped yellow petal with five notches at the tip. Insects are coaxed to these florets by a masterful lick of ultraviolet decoration on each petal, invisible to the human eye. But the clever dandelion does not need to rely just on pollination for its wide spread; it has evolved to have a backup reproductive process called apomixis, meaning it can fertilise seeds asexually and remove all chance from the affair.

When I was young, I, like many children, was delighted
to discover that when each floret on the dandelion sets
seed, it becomes a diaphanous sphere the size of a golf ball,
known as a dandelion clock. A fleeting, gossamer thing that
enchants with its airy grace, each seed attached delicately
to a parachute-like stalk and persuaded into flight with the
slightest puff of breath. The chute is comprised of bristles
known as pappus, made up of 100 filaments that increase
aerodynamic drag, helping to carry the seed kilometres from
the parent plant – an ancient secret of seed dispersal that
has sent countless children's wishes travelling far and wide.

A petal past midnight

The flower clock, or *horologium florae*, is a garden plan conceived
by the eminent Swedish botanist Carl Linnaeus, in his 1751 treatise
Philosophia Botanica. Linnaeus divided flowers into three categories:
meteorici open and close with the weather, *tropici* with the changing
hours of daylight, and *aequinoctales* with certain hours of the day.
The poetic suggestion is to plant flowers in the third category in
a clockface arrangement, to build a garden that can also tell the time.
The practicalities of this are lacking, but it is certainly a beautiful idea.

Fuchsia

FUCHSIA SPP. ———————— ONAGRACEAE

Fuchsias are native to South America and some Pacific Islands, including New Zealand where both a tree variety and a groundcover grow. The delicate hanging flowers are the main attraction. Their pendulous teardrop shape with four or more long petals surrounded by four sepals provides interesting two-tone combinations: the sepals bright red and petals purple, colours that attract pollinating hummingbirds.

All parts of the plant are edible. The fruit is sweet if fully ripe (try adding them to chutneys or muffins), while the leaves become more bitter as they age. The flowers taste slightly lemony, with the petals tastier than the surrounding sepals; it's best to remove the style and stamens inside. The simpler the flower, the more flavoursome it is likely to be, so avoid the large, frilly blossoms if you're growing plants to eat. Some growers have bred hybrids specifically for eating, with names like 'fuchsia berry' and 'gummiberry'.

Blossom granola

Fuchsia blossoms and berries are good additions to a bowl of crunchy breakfast granola. First, dry out 50 g (1¾ oz/1 cup) blossoms and 220 g (7¾ oz/1 cup) berries in a dehydrator or in an oven on its lowest setting. Then preheat an oven to 180° (360°F). Mix together 400 g (14 oz/4 cups) rolled (porridge) oats and 210 g (7⅓ oz/1½ cups) mixed nuts and seeds. Add 2 tablespoons coconut oil and 185 g (6½ oz/¼ cup) soft brown sugar, and a sprinkling of cardamom powder and rose water. Mix everything well, then transfer to a lined baking tray and bake for 15 minutes. Toss with a wooden spoon. Return the tray to the oven for another 5 minutes or so, until golden. Let the mix cool completely before adding the dried blossoms and berries, and store in an airtight container.

Summer

Love-in-a-mist

NIGELLA DAMASCENA ——————— RANUNCULACEAE

The delicate blue, pink and white flowers of love-in-a-mist – aptly named for their frothy, lace-like foliage – form an enchanting part of the summer garden. But it's the swollen, papery seed pods full of angular black seeds that have earned nigella its reputation as a general panacea, summed up by its Arabic name, *habbatul barakah*, meaning 'the seed of blessing'.

Inspiring many other poetic common names (bird's nest, blue spider flower, bride in hair, devil in the bush, blue crown and ragged lady), love-in-a-mist features in folklore associated with shapeshifting and love spells. A fable based on the 1190 death of Frederick I, the Holy Roman Emperor who led the Crusaders, tells how he drowned in Turkey's Göksu River after being seduced by a water spirit; afterwards, the riverbanks were covered with nigella flowers, growing from the green hairs of the nymph.

The ornamental garden variety is *Nigella damascena*; subtle flowers with colour stolen from the sky float with a collar of delicate misty bracts above fine plumy foliage. It features intriguing ornamental, balloon-shaped seed heads after flowering, which produce seeds with a spicy taste, though its cousin, *Nigella sativa*, is the species grown for its seed, known as black cumin and used as a condiment, a traditional medicine and to decorate baked goods. The seeds and petals of the ornamental *Nigella damascena* are both edible, which is somewhat surprising given it comes from the Ranunculaceae family, which tends to produce very poisonous substances – think of the deadly monkshood and hellebore plants, folkloric ingredients for sorceresses and witches. Love-in-a-mist is a halfway plant that seems to float between heaven and earth, poison and cure, the real and the spirit world.

The Miracle Garden

Love-in-a-mist has been at the root of the work of photographer Elspeth Diederix (1971–) for quite some time; her mysterious floral portraits demand a second look. A few years ago, Diederix built a laboratory for cultivating miracles: the Miracle Garden, a public, freely accessible studio in the beautiful Erasmuspark in Amsterdam-West. Diederix documents all the flowers she grows there and comments on them in an ever-growing archive of wonders. I am drawn to her image of a violently blue iris and a few blooms of love-in-a-mist that are almost exactly the same shade. An allium seed head bursts forth from the darkness of foliage like a firework you could hold in the palm of your hand.

Stargazer lily

LILIUM ORIENTALIS 'STARGAZER' ——————— LILIACEAE

While their ancestors have been admired and cultivated by humans for thousands of years, modern lilies are a complex amalgam of many species, crossed and hybridised to create myriad colours and patterns, growth habits and scents. 'Stargazer' is a common name often applied to all oriental hybrids, which descend from a number of liliums native to Japan and East Asia. They are all highly fragrant, with outward-facing flowers that appear to look up – hence the name stargazers.

In Japan and China, wild *Lilium* bulbs from many stargazer ancestors are harvested for food, a practice dating back many centuries. The name lily is a very popular one for garden plants, with many bearing it as their common name – calla lily, lily of the valley, toad lily, Peruvian lily, daylily, the list goes on and on – so it is important to note that the edible lilies are members of the genus *Lilium*. (Daylilies, *Hemerocallis*, are also edible and delicious; I talk about them on pages 170–3.)

The joy of a spot

One of the first things to bewitch me when I began drawing plants was the lurid and striking way they decorate themselves. Painterly splashes, dashes and dots adorn leaf and petal alike in intricate designs that seem almost too perfect to be real.

To me, a bejewelled starlet walking the red carpet cannot hold a candle to the luxury of a caladium leaf. The variety called Miss Muffet is resplendent in complementary blotches of blush pink and deep green – the colour combination of my dreams, and perhaps a gateway drug into a deep horticultural addiction.

My early works were a frenzy to record the most astounding and exotic patterning I could find, beguiled by nature's striking displays. The decorative leaves of begonias, and cymbidium and *Phalaenopsis* orchids, with their lurid cerise, lemon and carmine speckles – the gaudier, the more enamouring. Plain nasturtiums would not do for me – I had to illustrate the rarer variegated type. The markings on a celosia's leaves would send me into a state of agitation, with each leaf displaying a distinct combination of colours, shapes and textures. I could draw a plain lily, but the tiger lily held much more appeal!

For what reason? For whose eyes? Perhaps for the sheer delight of it.

The joy of patterns on petals and leaves is not just in their visual appeal, but also in the sense of mystery they evoke. Scientists have studied these patterns for years, trying to unravel the secrets of how they form and what purpose they serve. One theory is that the patterns help guide pollinators to the nectar and pollen they need to survive. Another theory suggests that the patterns help protect the flower from predators by confusing them and making it difficult for them to land on the petals.

Whatever the reason for the existence of patterns, whether we are admiring a field of wildflowers or the designs of an intricately cultivated garden, every unique petal is a reminder of the beauty and complexity of the natural world – something that fills me with a sense of wonder.

Common milkweed

ASCLEPIAS SYRIACA —————— APOCYNACEAE

Many people may agree with the characterisation given in *Asclepias syriaca*'s common name. One of more than 100 species of milkweed native to the Americas, and related to frangipani, oleander and hoyas, this tenacious plant reproduces via rhizomes underground, disrupting neat gardens, lawns and fields. It is seen by many as an irritant to be exterminated, often with toxic herbicide as it is very difficult to kill otherwise.

But milkweeds are increasingly becoming known for the important role they play in ecosystems. More than 450 insect species feed on *Asclepias syriaca*, including flies, beetles, ants, bees, wasps and butterflies. It is an important food source for the rapidly declining population of monarch butterfly caterpillars (*Danaus plexippus*). Monarch butterfly larvae consume only milkweeds, and in 2018 the US National Wildlife Federation connected the decline in their population to the reduction in milkweed.

While some species of milkweed are reputedly toxic, ethnobotanical records show that many Native American and Canadian First Nations tribes used several species for food: the stems can be cooked to season soups, or to eat like one would asparagus; the leaves can be cooked with meat or eaten raw; the dried latex can be made into chewing gum; and the seed pods can be boiled alone or with meat. Common milkweed flowers are edible and make a delightfully red fermented soda (follow the recipe for Wild fermented soda on page 96, replacing the elderflower with common milkweed).

How to plant a butterfly garden

Whether you have a huge yard or just a small balcony pot, consider planting flowers for beautiful butterflies to sip nectar from and plants for baby caterpillars to munch on. Plant a wide variety of flowers to cater to different species of butterflies. Ideally, this will mean your garden has blooms all year round. Research which butterfly-friendly plants are native to your area (milkweed might not be your best option). Brightly coloured, shallow and nectar-rich blossoms that like lots of sunshine are best – try planting them in large groups, so they're easy for butterflies to find.

Planting at different heights helps to attract butterflies. Use window boxes and hanging baskets to create variation (and to help with switching over flowers during seasons). Place some mushy, overripe fruit in a shallow dish as an alternative food source when there aren't as many flowers around, and a shallow dish of water will provide a drinking spot on hot days. Shady trees, shrubs and flat stones provide havens of cool and heat for butterflies. Tread very lightly when it comes to pest control – avoid pesticides!

Tuberose

AGAVE AMICA ——————— ASPARAGACEAE

While it would be nice to think the name tuberose celebrates this white, lily-like plant's sweet, floral scent, it refers more prosaically to its underground tubers. Related to asparagus and agave, the tuberose boasts a long stem that blooms into stunning star-shaped flowers. Native to Mexico – but no longer found in the wild – the showy, waxy flowers have a potent fragrance that has seduced noses all across the globe.

Reportedly cultivated by the Aztecs and possibly used to flavour their chocolate, tuberose has been used in perfumery since the seventeenth century, when its bulbs were first planted in the heart of the French perfume industry at Grasse. Said to be the most fragrant plant in the world, the tuberose's opulent scent continues to exude from the blossom even two days after picking, becoming even more compelling as night falls.

In Renaissance Italy, young women were prohibited from walking in gardens at night, lest the intoxicating scent of the tuberose inspire wanton thoughts. In India tuberoses are used as wedding decorations, and in Hawaii they're used in leis and flower garlands.

Enfleurage

Cold enfleurage is a meditative and delicate method for capturing the exquisite fragrances of fresh flowers at the height of their beauty. This traditional French method draws the scent molecules from a bloom and transforms them into a fat. Enfleurage is regarded as the strongest aromatic product in a perfumer's palette because of its high scent concentration and its ability to capture the most realistic version of a flower's scent.

The luxurious fat produced by enfleurage can be used as a solid perfume, in body balms and soaps, or refined further into a concentrated aromatic oil. Though it's no longer widely used by commercial perfumers due to its laborious nature, enfleurage is a tranquil technique, steeped in history.

Tuberose, lilac and gardenia – flowers that are effusive with scent, exhaling for many days after they have been plucked – are best suited to enfleurage. The scents of these delicate flowers are affected by heat, therefore they are not great candidates for other scent-extraction methods such as distillation.

Prepare flowers using the same process as for Alcoholic tincture on page 60.

You will need a fat (I suggest using vegetable fat, such as purified coconut oil or shea butter) and a shallow, wide tray or container – a baking tray works well – that will allow the fat to cover a large surface area.

Line the tray or container with about 1 cm (½ in) of fat. If your fat is too solid to spread at room temperature, gently melt the fat to make it easier to pour. If your fat is too liquid, warm the fat and add a small amount of beeswax. (Refrigeration may help the fat harden faster, but seal the container tightly so it does not absorb any unwanted scent.)

Scratch a crisscross pattern into the fat with a knife to increase the scent absorption.

Lightly place your blossoms on top of the fat, ensuring they are touching the fat but not submerged.

Cover the enfleurage to prevent contamination, but avoid sealing it airtight to prevent mould growth. Store away from heat and sunlight. In warmer environments, refrigeration might be best.

When the flowers start to lose their vibrancy or scent, remove them with tweezers.

Repeat this process, replacing the flowers until the fat has a luscious level of scent. Some flowers may need to be refreshed upwards of six times! You can test a small sample of the fat on your skin using a skewer. To inhibit mould growth, never use your hands when working with the fat.

When the fat has reached your desired scent level, transfer the finished pomade into a sterilised jar and squeeze out any trapped air. Store the pomade in the refrigerator to keep the scent potent.

Hops

HUMULUS LUPULUS —————— CANNABACEAE

Native to Eurasia, hops has been used for millennia, and is, I think, one of the most widely consumed yet little-known flowers, sneaking into our favourite alcoholic beverages without us even knowing what it looks like. Hops is best known for adding a bitter taste to beer – it is just one of many herbs used for this over the centuries – but in the Middle Ages brewers discovered that it also acts as a preservative, preventing beer from going off. By 1710 the English parliament had banned the use of non-hop bitters, and set a penny-per-pound hop tax to benefit from the monopoly. Now hundreds of varieties of hops are grown, each with an individual flavour and aroma. Some are boiled for a long time and others are thrown into the ferment at the last minute like a citrusy garnish.

The origin of the plant's common name comes from the Anglo-Saxon *hoppen,* meaning 'to climb', while its pleasing botanical name refers to the Latin *humus* for 'soil' and *lupulus* meaning 'little wolf', which describes its voracious growth. A rapacious perennial that produces twining vines (technically called bines), hops will grab hold of any tree branch or shrubbery within reach. Since the eighteenth century, hops has been grown in 'hopyards', climbing frames that were tended by men on stilts before machines could do the job.

The plant has leaves that inexplicably change shape as they age, but the part used most often is the dried, cone-like female flower, which contains a gland that secretes resins and antibacterial essential oils similar to those of cannabis, which is unsurprisingly in the same plant family. Early colonisers in the United States found multiple uses for hops: young spring shoots were eaten like asparagus; a wax extracted from the tendrils was used as a dye; the fibres were used like flax to make textiles; stalks were used in basketry; and spent hops were fed to sheep. Hops contain some toxins, however, and are particularly poisonous to dogs. Some people have an allergic reaction to the sap, while beer drinkers can get a sore throat, swollen tongue or skin rash from beers with high levels of hop oils.

Golden hop milk

Hops flowers are known for calming nerves and promoting relaxation. They are used in this golden milk recipe, which makes a comforting beverage, enough for two or three people.

In a small saucepan, combine 500 ml (17 fl oz/2 cup) milk of any kind, 1 teaspoon ground turmeric, 1 teaspoon ground ginger (you can substitute either with fresh), ½ teaspoon ground cinnamon and 1 tablespoon coconut oil. You can also add other spices, such as cardamom, vanilla and black pepper. Add honey to taste, along with a small handful of fresh or dried hops flowers. Stir gently over medium heat until it starts simmering, then strain and serve.

Bellflower

CAMPANULA LATIFOLIA —————— CAMPANULACEAE

From wind-blasted alpine outcrops where tiny plants are no bigger than the individual flowers on the grand spires of their American cousins, to sunny meadows and the subtropics of Africa and Asia, the *Campanula* genus is one of the most varied in the world, with more than 430 varieties. The shape of the plant's flowers explains its common and Latin names, but it has several other affectionate nicknames, including fairy thimbles and bats-in-the-belfry. The bellflower has huge value as a garden plant, and some larger species are grown for cut flowers, but it also has a long history of use in folk medicine, particularly in Russia and Italy.

Rampion (*Campanula rapunculus*) was once widely grown in Europe for its leaves, which were eaten in salads or used like spinach, and for its turnip-like roots, which are spicy like radishes. In the Grimm brothers fairytale, Rapunzel was named for this plant, which her mother had craved so much during pregnancy that her father stole it from the witch's garden next door.

Floral meditation

To truly appreciate the beauty and wonder of a flower, it is important to approach it with a sense of openness and presence. Begin by finding a quiet place where you can sit or stand comfortably, and take a few deep breaths to centre yourself.

As you turn your attention to the flower, allow your gaze to soften and become receptive. Let go of any thoughts or distractions and simply observe the flower as it is, without judgement or expectation.

Notice the delicate petals, vibrant colours and intricate patterns that make up its unique form. Take in the scent, and let it fill your senses with its fragrance. Appreciate the way the flower moves in the breeze, and how it interacts with the environment.

As you continue to gaze at the flower, consider the life cycle that brought it to this moment. Think about the seed that first germinated, the soil and nutrients that nourished its growth, and the sun and rain that sustained it.

Reflect on the interconnectedness of all living things, and how this single flower is part of a larger ecosystem. Consider the role it plays in the web of life, and how it contributes to the wellbeing of the planet.

As you conclude your meditation, take a moment to express gratitude for the gift of this flower, and for the natural world that sustains us all.

Nasturtium

TROPAEOLUM MAJUS —————— TROPAEOLACEAE

A mainstay of cottage and herb gardens, the nasturtium likely originated in Bolivia and Peru. The flower's bright-hued, trump-shaped blooms speckled Claude Monet's central path at Giverny, and its pungent odour inspired its common name – *nasus* meaning 'a nose', and *tortus* meaning 'twisted'. The genus name is derived from the Greek word, meaning 'trophy', and can be credited to prolific Swedish naturalist Carl Linnaeus. The rounded leaves and blooms, Linnaeus observed, resembled the circular shields and bloodstained helmets that soldiers once seized as trophies on the battlefield.

The flowers, leaves, seeds, pods and buds of this prolific canary creeper are edible and have a strong, peppery bite similar to watercress, making them very good for pesto. The seeds and buds can be pickled like capers.

Every year since 1904 the Isabella Stewart Gardner Museum in Boston has celebrated the return of spring, and the birthday of its namesake and founder, with a hanging nasturtium display. Each April more than 100 vines cascade over the grand windows, balconies and arches salvaged by Stewart Gardner from Venetian palazzos to create her own unique vision of an interior courtyard, with rotating floral displays at the heart of the museum. The spectacular exhibit is in place for only a brief moment but takes a year of planning, with the nasturtiums carefully tended to by the museum's horticulturalists throughout the bitter Boston winter. The annual event sees this humble cottage garden plant upstaging a priceless collection of art with an outpouring of vibrant beauty.

Nasturtium pesto

Nasturtium is a generous plant, reseeding easily and popping up everywhere. When I have a glut of nasturtiums, I like to pickle the fresh green seeds as a caper substitute or make a vibrant pesto.

To make a pesto, wash 200 g (7 oz/2 cups) nasturtium leaves and 100 g (3½ oz/1 cup) nasturtium flowers. Use unblemished leaves and flowers. Blend the leaves and flowers with 3 cloves of garlic, 225 g (8 oz/1½ cups) pine nuts or pistachios, and 150 g (5¼ oz/1½ cups) grated parmesan. While the ingredients are blending, add 375 ml (12¾ fl oz/1½ cups) olive oil in a steady stream. Continue blending until a smooth paste forms. Store in the fridge with a small layer of olive oil on top to prevent the pesto from oxidising, and use within 2 weeks.

Carnation

DIANTHUS CARYOPHYLLUS ———————— CARYOPHYLLACEAE

Visitors to Greece and the Balkans may know the pleasure of walking in rocky, dry hills and being greeted by wildflowers familiar from gardens around the world: thyme, crocus, narcissus – and pretty pink dianthus, one of the original species that larger modern carnations were bred from.

Commonly called pinks, or clove pinks because of their scent, it is possible that the colour pink was named for these plants. The name 'pinking shears', for scissors that cut with a zigzag pattern, may derive from the plant, too, referring to the tooth-like dissections on the petal edges. *Dianthus* means 'flower of the gods'.

Carnation petals have a sweet, spicy scent and the flowers are believed to be one of the ingredients in the secret recipe for French herbal liqueur Chartreuse. In Elizabethan times they were used to make spiced wine, beer and tea, and were used as a tonic for everything from stress to travel sickness. The flowers can also be used to flavour vinegar and sauces, and to decorate salads and desserts, but remove the white petal bases first as these are bitter. The rest of the plant should not be eaten and can be toxic for pets.

The paper garden

Artist Mary Granville Delany (1700–1788) bloomed at seventy-two, when she noticed a scarlet geranium petal against her ebony table and a piece of paper exactly the same colour. This discovery sparked her life's work: *Flora Delanica*, 985 botanical masterpieces she created using Indian ink, tissue paper, wallpaper remnants and flower parts, considered by some to be the first mixed-media collages. Her intricate reproductions caught the eye of King George III and his wife, Queen Charlotte, themselves amateur botanists. I am particularly enamoured by her depictions of more humble flowers, such as the lovely carnation.

Passionflower

PASSIFLORA SPP. ———————— PASSIFLORACEAE

Other-worldly and wild, the sculptural, vivid blooms of the passionflower vine undoubtedly inspire just that – passion from many admirers. Native to the humid forests of Florida, Mexico's Yucatán Peninsula, the islands of the Caribbean and the jungles of Central America, passionflowers flourish all over the tropics, from Australia's north coast to the steamy jungles of Vietnam.

Their name is not derived from ardent emotion but rather from Christian mythology. Spanish missionaries arriving in the Americas in the sixteenth century used all parts of the plant to teach Indigenous populations the story of Christ's death and rebirth. The purple colour of the petals was related to the season of Lent, the five sepals and petals combined represented the ten apostles (excluding Judas the betrayer and Peter the denier), the circle of filaments was the crown of thorns, the three stigmas symbolised the three nails used to nail Christ to the cross, the five anthers represented the five wounds he suffered, the three-lobed leaves represented the holy trinity, and the plant's tendrils were said to represent the whips used to flagellate Christ as he carried the cross.

This flower, inspiring so much feeling among Christians and so distinctive due to its reproductive parts, attracts a diverse range of pollinators from bees to hummingbirds to bats.

Passionflower bitters

Passionflower bitters are believed to have calming properties and may help to ease anxiety and promote relaxation. Add a few drops of passionflower bitters to your favourite cocktails, mocktails or seltzer water to enhance their flavour and complexity.

Put 2 tablespoons dried passionflower (*Passiflora incarnata*), 1 tablespoon dried chamomile flowers, and 1 tablespoon dried lavender flowers into a jar. Add 1 tablespoon dried orange peel and 1 tablespoon dried lemon peel, along with 1 tablespoon dried ginger root, 1 tablespoon dried allspice berries, 1 tablespoon dried cardamom pods, 1 tablespoon dried juniper berries, and 2 sticks of cinnamon. Optionally, you can add 1 tablespoon dried gentian root for bitterness, or 1 tablespoon granulated sugar or honey for sweetness, depending on your preference. Lastly, pour in 500 ml (17 fl oz/2 cups) high-proof vodka or a rectified spirit like Everclear (at least 100-proof).

Store the jar at room temperature and allow the ingredients to infuse for 21 days, shaking every other day. Once the mixture is infused, strain the contents of the jar through muslin (cheesecloth) into dropper bottles. The bitters can be stored indefinitely, but the flavour may evolve over time.

Fig

FICUS CARICA —————— MORACEAE

You may have arrived at this page confused by my inclusion of the humble fig in a book filled with flowers, but fear not, gentle reader: take a bite of a fig and your mouth will be brimming with a thick carpet of minuscule blossoms, or florets. They are indeed flowers. We never actually observe the blossoms of a fig tree. They are shy flowers that bloom meekly inwards, confined in an empty pouch called a syconium, far from the flamboyance of other blooms. Only once they are fertilised and their ovaries become fleshy are they truly a fruit.

The fig and its fertility-related stories have featured in many cultures of the Middle and Near East, where it has been cultivated for at least 4000 years. The botanical story of the fig is one of sex: the fig 'fruit' can be either male or female, and its relationship with its pollinator, a tiny female wasp, is so profound that it is one of the most widely known instances of species-specific coevolution.

Flowers and pollinators

The tale of the fig and the wasp is one of 60 million years of symbiosis; neither could exist without the other. Understanding this partnership is helpful in comprehending the delicate interplay between flowers and their pollinators. A fig is a sealed orb of florets that needs to be pollinated to produce offspring. Its syconia is secured against any insect that tries to enter, lured by its sweet scent – all but the tiny female fig wasp.

At the beginning of the season, fig trees develop their timid inverted flowers with sterile florets but a few male ones near the opening of the syconium. The tiny female wasp enters and lays eggs in some of the infertile florets, which bulge with the growing pupae like a canker. For the wasp mother, this fig is now her tomb: her wings are destroyed when she enters the fig, and she will perish inside. The male larvae emerge first, to seek females in the florets and fertilise them. Once their job is done they will die, their short life span completed within the body of the flower. The young females hatch, and their exit from the syconium forces them into contact with the pollen-bearing male flowers at its rim.

As the season progresses, fig trees produce flowers with female florets. Female fig wasps, laden with pollen from the male florets, follow the alluring scent of these blossoms and, compelled by nature, endeavour to lay their eggs. But unlike the male flowers, the female florets are incompatible with the anatomy of the wasp, and she cannot lay eggs in them. Pollination of the flower has been assured, however: the industrious wasp has transferred the pollen from her legs onto the waiting stigmas.

In this extraordinary example of symbiosis, nearly every different species of fig has its own particular species of wasp, attuned to its specific pollination needs. (This is in nature – most figs in commercial cultivation do not require pollination.) The relationship between the fig and the wasp, honed into remarkable efficiency over many millennia, puts the haphazard strategies of other plants to shame, most of which leave the delicate dance of pollination to chance and the wind.

Queen Anne's lace

DAUCUS CAROTA ——————— APIACEAE

A Eurasian plant with a white lacy inflorescence in the form of a flat-topped umbel, Queen Anne's lace is not native to North America, where it is a commonly encountered roadside weed. It can be distinguished from many poisonous relatives that have a similar appearance, like hemlock, by the long forked bracts beneath the flower head. It is sometimes referred to as wild carrot because its whitish taproot is purported to be the wild ancestor of our cultivated carrots.

The evocative common name is derived from the appearance of the inflorescence, with its tiny white flowers resembling a white lace doily – often with a dark red to blackish spot (flower) in the centre, said to represent a drop of blood that fell on lace being made by Queen Anne of England when she pricked her finger with a needle.

Umbels

An umbel is a flat-topped or ball-shaped inflorescence (a cluster of flowers on a stem) with extended pedicels (the stems that attach single flowers to an inflorescence) that grow from a central stem like the ribs of an umbrella. These flowers are typical of the plant family Apiaceae, which was previously called Umbelliferae. The word umbel comes from the Latin *umbella*, meaning 'sunshade' – which of course is where the modern term umbrella is derived from. The umbels of Queen Anne's lace are typical examples, their complex filigree structures a fusion of umbels on umbels – each ray features a smaller umbellet at its tip.

Members of the Apiaceae family have been cultivated by humans for millennia because of their generous and important crops, including carrot, parsnip, parsley, fennel, caraway, dill and anise. Some are revered and feared alike for their sinister qualities – hemlock produces a rather lethal toxin, but to the untrained eye it passes easily for the umbels of Queen Anne's lace.

Bronze fennel

FOENICULUM VULGARE 'PURPUREUM' —————— APIACEAE

Silent fireworks you can hold in the palm of your hand, tender fennel flowers are small florets that grow in exploding clusters to form a delicate bouquet in the most happy shade of bright yellow.

Fennel is in the umbel family, along with carrots and coriander. There are two types of fennel – bronze fennel being a herb, and Florence fennel a vegetable (known for its bulbs) – both with dreamy feathery foliage like the fronds of dill. Bronze fennel is a highly attractive plant and desirable to all the insect pollinators around. It will become the life force of your garden or balcony, drawing bees, butterflies and hoverflies galore, thrumming and dancing with constant insect activity.

With a taste similar to licorice, fennel flowers are used as flavouring in cooking and for medicinal purposes. Fennel pollen, dried and dusted, adds a most fragrant sweetness to a dish. The fresh green seeds are also surprisingly sweet. Drying the inflorescences and saving the seed may seem like a tedious task when you can buy a bag for a few dollars, but I find it quite meditative.

Fennel pollen ice cream

My favourite way to enjoy fennel pollen is in a sweet dish, such as this luscious ice cream.

Combine 190 ml (6½ fl oz/1¾ cups) thick cream (double/heavy), 3 strips lemon zest, 1 teaspoon fennel pollen and ½ teaspoon salt in a saucepan and bring to a boil. Remove from the heat and discard the lemon zest. Whisk 2 large eggs with 160 ml (5½ fl oz/⅔ cup) agave nectar in a heatproof bowl, then slowly pour in the cream mix, whisking constantly. Pour the mixture back into the saucepan and cook over a medium–low heat, stirring constantly, until slightly thickened. Do not boil.

Pour the mixture through a fine-mesh sieve into a heatproof bowl, then cool to room temperature, stirring occasionally. Chill in the refrigerator, then freeze in an ice-cream freezer according to the manufacturer's instructions.

Sunchoke

HELIANTHUS TUBEROSUS ——————— ASTERACEAE

Sunchokes, also known as Jerusalem artichokes or earth apples, are a tall, fast-growing species of sunflower native to North America. Their prolific tubers made them an excellent, reliable food source for First Nations people, and early explorers eagerly brought them back to Europe, where they also grew well – to the point that herbalist John Parkinson wrote in 1629 that what had once been a delicacy reserved for the queen had become so common and cheap 'that even the most vulgar begin to despise them'.

A member of the daisy family, the sunchoke, whose botanical name *Helianthus* comes from the Ancient Greek for sun, is a composite or ray flower, like its close relative the larger, showier sunflower, *Helianthus annuus*. The flower head is composed of hundreds of individual florets, flowers of two types. Those with a single long petal (the ray florets) surround those with tiny tubular petals (the disc florets) that make up the interior face of the flower. The very clever result of this grouping is to attract more pollinators; they also come to maturity at different times, ensuring a great success rate of fertilisation. The clever sunchoke composite flower has a pleasant nutty flavour, much like its tuber.

Sunchoke flower kombucha

This kombucha is infused with the nutty, unusual sunchoke flavour but could be made with any number of edible flower combinations – try rose, elderflower, chamomile or violet. Just be sure the flower has a strong flavour. This recipe makes 2 litres (68 fl oz/8 cups).

Bring 250 g (8¾ oz/1¼ cups) sugar and 250 ml (8½ fl oz/1 cup) water to boil in a medium pot, stirring to dissolve the sugar. Remove from the heat and add 500 ml (17 fl oz/2 cups) more water to cool it down fast. Once the sugar syrup cools to room temperature, transfer it to a blender with 200 g (7 oz/4 cups) sunchoke flower petals and blend until they are finely chopped. Transfer the liquid to a container, cover and refrigerate for at least 8 hours.

The following day strain the flower syrup through a fine-mesh sieve into a sterilised jar. Stir in 200 ml (7 fl oz/¾ cup) unpasteurised kombucha, then carefully place a scoby (fermentation starter) into the liquid. Cover the vessel with muslin (cheesecloth) and set in a warm place.

Leave the kombucha to ferment, checking it each day. When you are happy with the flavour of your kombucha, probably in about a week, transfer the scoby to a small, open-mouthed container for storage (covered with some of your kombucha to keep it alive). Strain your kombucha into sterilised bottles and store in the fridge.

Amaranth

AMARANTHUS CAUDATUS —————— AMARANTHACEAE

Farmers may know amaranth as a pigweed that is poisonous to cattle; gardeners may recognise it as the dramatic bedding plant love-lies-bleeding; and some foodies and foragers may regard it as a superfood with many possible uses. Amaranth inflorescences are pleasingly bedraggled plumes that hang in sculptural panicles, each comprised of hundreds, if not thousands, of minuscule burgundy or crimson florets. These florets mature into tiny, nutritionally excellent seeds – easily 50,000 per plant.

Amaranth leaves, seeds and roots have been used as effective traditional medicine across Asia, Africa and the Americas, although species can accumulate poisonous levels of nitrates in artificially fertilised soils. Amaranth was one of five essential plants in the diets of the Aztecs, Incans and Mayans, and evidence of its use goes back at least 6000 years. As well as eating the broad, deeply veined leaf, they used the seeds to make a drink, ground it for flour, and mixed it with honey or agave to mould figures of deities. By eating the flesh of the gods, believers thought they would be instilled with their power and spirit. Because of this religious association, Spanish colonisers banned growing or eating amaranth, but the practice now forms part of the Mexican Day of the Dead celebrations.

The name is derived from the Greek for 'unfading', referring to the long-lasting flowers. In medieval Europe, the amaranth, whose Latin name evokes words connoting love, became known as *flos amoris*, meaning flower of love. The nineteenth century saw Victorians adopt the drooping, scarlet amaranth as a symbol of unrequited affection, hence the name love-lies-bleeding.

Natural dye

Amaranth is an excellent natural source of charming pink-toned dyes for fabric. In particular the variety Hopi Red Dye is a traditional amaranth grown for generations by the Hopi as a dye plant. The Hopi also use the deep red flower bract to colour their world-renowned piki bread. Amaranth Hopi Red Dye can easily be grown from seed.

When working with natural dyes, it is best to use a natural yarn or fabric such as linen, wool, silk or cotton. The fabric will need to be treated with a mordant such as aluminium sulphate before dying; you can learn more about this process in *Wild Colour* by Jenny Dean.

To use Hopi Red Dye, place both the seed heads and leaves of the plant, about 150 g (5¼ oz) in total, in a large pot and cover with tap water. Heat the pot slowly to 60° (140°F) and keep at that temperature for an hour, then let the pot sit for a few days to fully extract the colour. Strain out the plant matter and then add your material. Reheat to 60° (140°F) for an hour to dye the fabric. You can reuse the dye bath until the colour has been exhausted. Colours can range from dark salmon to shades of orange, red and pink depending on the intensity of the dye.

Other plants and flowers to experiment with include avocado pips, onion skins, weld, coreopsis, dahlias, sulfur cosmos, marigolds, sunflowers and dyer's chamomile.

Slow and gentle is the best method when working with natural dyes – it is easy to overheat the dye bath and dull or change the colour. If you are not able to extract enough colour from the plants with lower temperatures, you can increase the heat or leave the dye stuff in the pot on the stove for longer.

Daylily

HEMEROCALLIS SPP. ——————— ASPHODELACEAE

The evanescent flower of the daylily opens under the glare of the summer morning sun, creating a dazzling display – just, as its name suggests, for that one single day alone. The second part of its common name, however, is ripe for confusion: *Hemerocallis* are not true lilies and have fallen victim to one of the many upheavals in scientific botanical classification in recent years. In 2009 they were removed from the Liliaceae family of true lilies, with which they share a very similar shape.

This edible plant has a distinguished cultural background. Native to China and Japan, where it has grown wild for millennia, it has been used as a veritable pharmacopoeia to treat different ailments. This multidimensional plant is bent on giving good value. Dried daylily blossoms, called *gum jum choi* in Chinese, can be used like okra to thicken soup; fresh, they can be dipped in batter and fried or eaten raw, and are said to have a peppery aftertaste. In late spring the tender heart of the plant can be blanched and eaten like asparagus.

This sturdy plant will happily leapfrog out of the cultivated garden and establish itself on roadsides and in fields due to its ease of propagation. The original range of yellows and bright oranges of the wild daylily has exploded in scope with the advent of modern hybridisation. Daylily hybrids have reached the dizzying number of 35,000 in a testament to their popularity.

Painting with flowers

In a perfect combination of art and nature, you can use the petals of almost any vibrant flower to make your own paints. To make a lake pigment, you combine the colour compounds present in flowers with a mordant, which is a substance that helps fix the colour onto a substrate like paper or fabric.

To embark on this creative journey, you'll need some materials to hand:

- fresh and colourful flower petals such as daylily petals
- alum (aluminium potassium sulphate)
- warm water
- washing soda (sodium carbonate)
- a pot for simmering
- a stirring rod or spoon
- a blender
- paper coffee filters
- a mortar and pestle, or a coffee grinder
- a glass or plastic container for pigment storage.

Begin by preparing the flower petals for the pigment-making process. Dissolve alum in warm water – the typical weight ratio is 10:1 flower petals to alum. (For example, if you have 100 g (3½ oz) flower petals, use 10 g (⅓ oz) alum.) Stir the mixture until the alum is fully dissolved. Submerge the flower petals in the alum solution, ensuring they are fully covered by the liquid. Soak the petals in the solution for at least 24 hours to fix the colour and enhance the lightfastness of the pigment.

Blend the petals and the alum solution, then pour the blended mixture into a pot. Simmer (do not boil) the mixture for approximately 1–2 hours, stirring occasionally. If the mixture starts to become too thick, add a little more water.

Dissolve 1 tablespoon washing soda in 100 ml (3½ fl oz/⅓ cup) warm water. Gradually add the dissolved washing soda to your petal and alum solution until it foams up. (This step adjusts the liquid pH to better bind the colour to the substrate.) Let the liquid sit undisturbed for a few hours or overnight. The lake pigment will precipitate and settle at the bottom of the container.

Carefully strain the liquid through a double layer of 2 coffee filters. Once strained, air-dry the pigment on the filter. This may take some time – it needs to lose all its moisture to be suitable for storage and use.

When the pigment has thoroughly dried, grind it into a fine powder using a mortar and pestle or a coffee grinder. Store in a glass or plastic container with an airtight lid, and protect it from moisture, direct sunlight and heat.

Lake pigments can be the beginning of many artistic projects, from painting to dyeing fabrics. To transform the dry pigment into paint, mix it with gum arabic to your desired consistency.

Zinnia

ZINNIA ELEGANS ———————— ASTERACEAE

There are few more reliable summer blooms in a garden or vase than zinnias. Their composite flowers gush with colour and offer a dazzling array of choice – petals saturated with rose, chartreuse, yellow, orange, red, purple or lilac. Always abuzz with bees and a magnet for other pollinators, including butterflies and hummingbirds, zinnias ask very little of their garden caretakers and give so much. Native to the dry grasslands of the Americas, these daisies are an easy-care plant for warm climates. Experiments on the International Space Station have proven it's even possible for zinnias to grow and bloom in space.

Spaniards colonising Mexico called the small native zinnias *mal de ojos*, meaning 'eyesore', apparently finding them ugly. Mexican artist Frida Kahlo seems to have disagreed, featuring them in many of her paintings. Zinnia petals are edible but taste quite bitter, so are best used as a garnish.

Cheerful flowers to grow with ease

Easy annuals are simple to grow from seed, perennials require little care and return year after year, and bulbs are practically foolproof when planted properly. All attract pollinators and require little fertiliser or water. Aside from zinnias, here are some others to start with.

- sunflower
- cosmos
- nasturtium
- marigold
- coneflower
- geranium
- daffodil
- daylily

Sweet pea

LATHYRUS ODORATUS ———— FABACEAE

Looking at the wide range of colour combinations in modern sweet pea varieties, and considering their popularity around the world, it's hard to believe that the original species was always purple and pink and grew only in Italy. A Sicilian monk was so taken with the sweet pea that he sent the seeds abroad. Scottish horticulturist Henry Eckford led the way in breeding modern varieties, and a sweet pea show is still held in his honour each year. A strain of large, frilly flowers called Spencer varieties was developed at the family home of Princess Diana.

Sweet peas are grown mostly for their scented flowers, which last well as cut flowers and generously produce more blooms the more they're picked. However, unlike edible peas, sweet peas are toxic, so it's important to keep track of different peas grown in the garden! Sweet peas have hairier seed pods, and edible peas usually have white flowers.

Common poisonous flowers

It astonishes me that so many of the plants around us are downright deadly, some as common as weeds. Who would have thought that the humble buttercup can be lethal to cattle? That the leaves of foxglove might benefit a heart patient in the right dose but would otherwise kill them? Deadly nightshade provides a warning in its name, as long as you can recognise it. And the flowers of a tomato – a plant in the same family as deadly nightshade – carry toxins. Hemlock, the substance Socrates was forced to drink when he was sentenced to death in 399 BCE, bears a striking resemblance to Queen Anne's lace; it is important for foragers to know the difference.

Given the growing obsession with floral garnishes and edible flowers, I'm further astonished by how often I see poisonous blooms finding their way onto plates. A florist friend was recently served a cake adorned by the rather sweet purple and white blossoms of *Duranta* – an exceptionally toxic member of the nightshade family, and a very common garden plant in Australia. The flowers made her rather ill, but luckily she escaped death – and the horrible irony of being the florist who died from eating a flower.

This list is a starting point for common poisonous plants, but *always* do your research before adding a flower to your cake or cocktail.

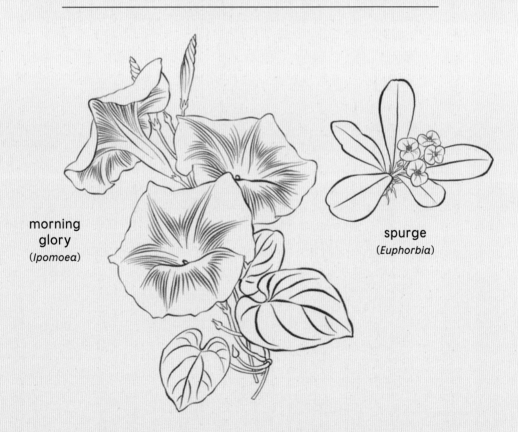

morning
glory
(*Ipomoea*)

spurge
(*Euphorbia*)

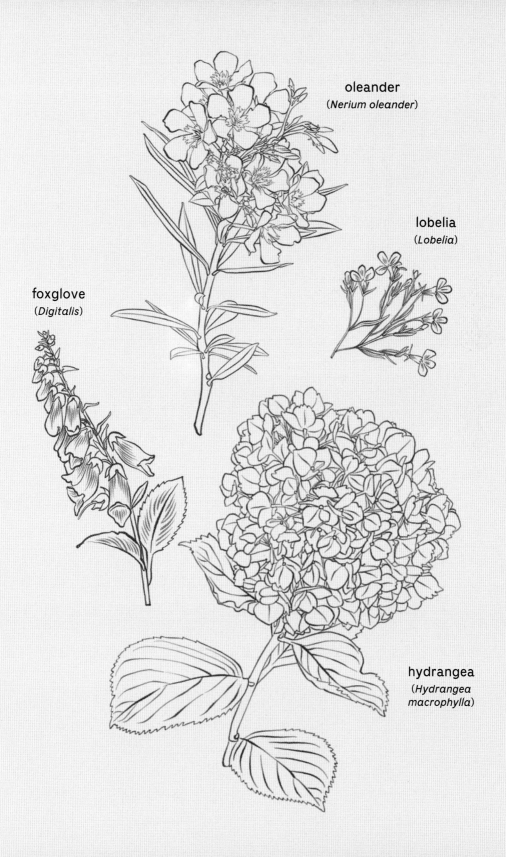

oleander
(*Nerium oleander*)

lobelia
(*Lobelia*)

foxglove
(*Digitalis*)

hydrangea
(*Hydrangea macrophylla*)

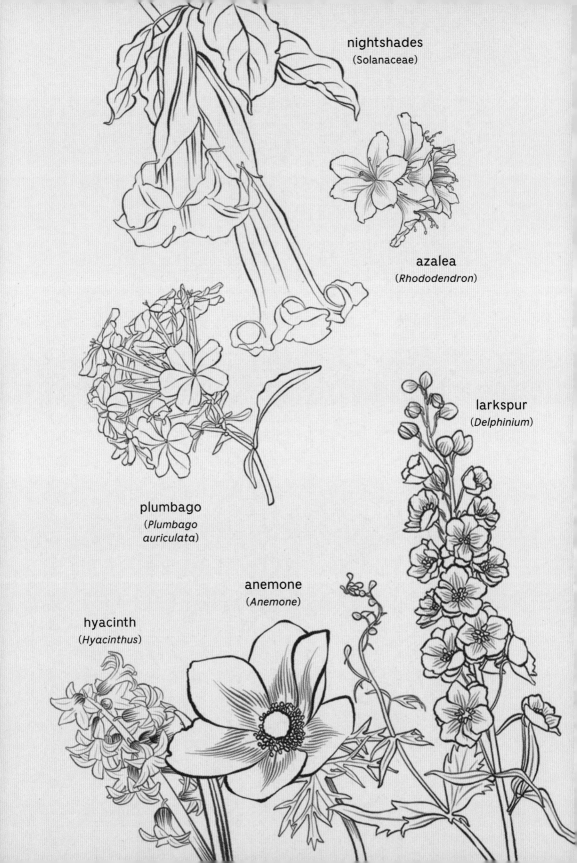

nightshades
(Solanaceae)

azalea
(*Rhododendron*)

larkspur
(*Delphinium*)

plumbago
(*Plumbago
auriculata*)

anemone
(*Anemone*)

hyacinth
(*Hyacinthus*)

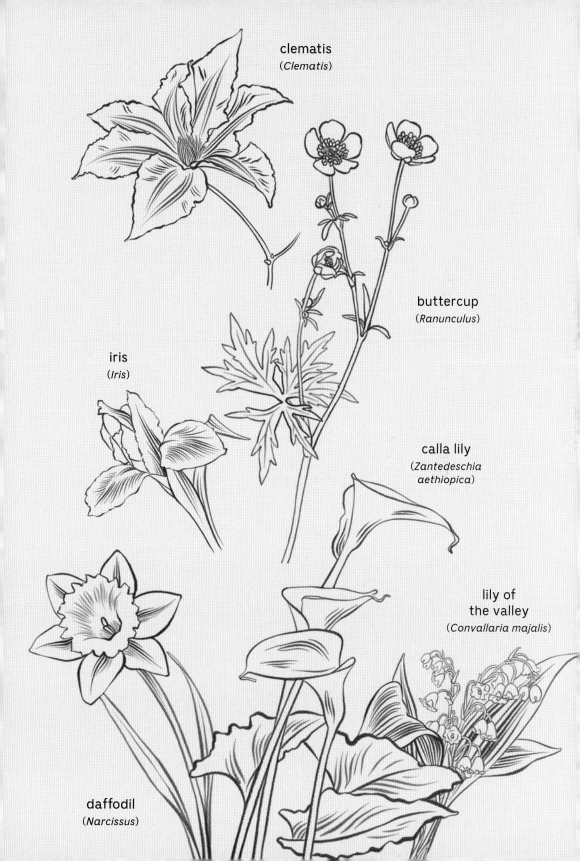

clematis
(*Clematis*)

buttercup
(*Ranunculus*)

iris
(*Iris*)

calla lily
(*Zantedeschia aethiopica*)

lily of
the valley
(*Convallaria majalis*)

daffodil
(*Narcissus*)

Dahlia

DAHLIA SPP. ———————— ASTERACEAE

The plant we know as the dahlia is the national flower of Mexico, but there it is called *cocoxochitl*, meaning 'flower of hollow stems with water'. The ancient Aztecs relied on it as a source of food and water, and also used it as a medicine, specifically for treating epilepsy. The tubers, akin to sweet potatoes, can be dried and stored, and the flowers used as edible decorations. The long, hollow stem of the giant tree dahlia (*Dahlia imperialis*) was used by the Aztecs to transport water.

Forty-one dahlia species grow across Mexico's mountainous areas and into Central and South America, and, from these, hundreds of modern cultivars have been bred. Some are as curvaceous as half-dressed women in a Rubens painting, others as spiky as sea creatures or cacti, and still others feature uncountable petals jammed close together in a pompom-like fashion. They are conspicuous and assertive and vulgar. They shoot up to monumental heights. I love their colours and their willingness to bloom until the absolute last vestige of summer has been squeezed out.

Dahlias were first brought to Europe by Spanish explorers in 1570. The name dahlia was chosen in 1791 to honour Swedish botanist Anders Dahl, but in 1805 an argument over naming arose, with a German botanist calling the plant georgina instead – it is still known as georgina in Russia. Marie Antoinette was an admirer, as was Claude Monet, and Bedřich Smetana, a Czech composer, wrote the *Dahlia polka*. In 1846 the Royal Caledonian Horticultural Society of Edinburgh offered £2000 to the first person to create a blue dahlia. So far, no one has achieved this.

A renewed interest in edible flowers has seen many growers taste-test different dahlias, with mixed reviews – the flavour of some is compared to carrots, apples or water chestnuts, and others are described as more astringent and bitter. A range of dahlia recipes can now be found, including for ice cream, chips, soup and as an addition to cakes.

Arranging flowers

It will come as no great surprise that I approach flower arranging in the same way I compose a painting or a drawing. Making art, for me, is just arranging flowers on a page after all. There must be drama, flair and general abundance. Above all, it must tug at the heartstrings.

Dahlias are the poster child for overt and luscious abundance. In their short season they gift us with an embarrassment of riches – masses of vibrant colour, texture, shape and form. One plant is covered in a plethora of blooms. It would be a travesty to display them in a way other than en masse as nature intended. Use them when they are in season and gloriously cheap, like you would a glut of good tomatoes: often and with great generosity, celebrating the bounty of what summer brings.

In the world of competitive dahlia growing, symmetry is everything. Flowers are judged on their perfection of form. Pompom, ball and cactus types are preferred, and growers dedicate their lives to growing a medal winner. But these are not what I am drawn to – I'd rather the wilder versions, those that are big, blousy and Rubenesque, full of movement and imperfect form.

They have become ubiquitous now, but the variety Cafe au Lait is a perennial favourite of mine to draw and arrange. No ribbons for symmetry will ever be won here, but gosh they create such interesting movement and drama in a vase. I have a mantel at home I like to load to bursting with as many blooms as will fit. I think of the joy those dahlias will bring each time someone walks into the room, the air sucked out by flowers, their eye and heart unable to focus on anything else. That is the life I want to live, filled to the brim with beauty.

My arrangement style is haphazard but rigorously considered. I want it to look effortlessly perfect and perfectly imperfect at the same time. Nature needs little intervention, so follow its lead closely. Pick grasses and weeds from the side of the road to accompany your hothouse-grown blooms, adding an element of whimsy. Let this book and your eye guide you to what is in season.

Also be guided by the greats – I like to take inspiration from the wild, lush and abundant floral paintings of the Dutch masters who often used diagonal lines in their compositions to create a sense of movement. By arranging the dahlias so that they are not all standing upright, but instead so that some are leaning or bending in different directions, you can create a sense of vitality. The eye drawn by angles around the composition.

Leave room for air, for negative space – room for the little birds to fly through. What to leave out of a composition is often more important that what to include. The Dutch masters left parts of their paintings blank to draw the viewer's eye to a focal point, giving the flowers room to breathe. I use this technique in my own art for the same effect.

Hollyhock and mallow

ALCEA SPP. ———————— MALVACEAE

Hollyhocks and their hibiscus cousins are the poster children for a huge family of plants that includes some very diverse and imperceptibly related members – crops such as okra, cotton, cacao, durian and many ornamentals. The common name mallow comes from its Latin name, *malva*, which also gave us the word mauve. The stone malachite was named because it had the same green colour as mallow leaves.

A few tall spires of cheerful hollyhocks aflame with blooms can instantly convey an English cottage garden look, but most mallow are native to Eurasia, and the common hollyhock was introduced to England from China. They grow easily from seed and are listed on the Invasive Plant Atlas of the United States register; the native cousin *Iliamna rivularis* makes a great replacement in the United States.

As with many mallows, the leaves are edible although often quite hairy. Marshmallows that you roast over campfires got their name from the marshmallow plant *Althaea officinalis*, because the gluey mucilage in its roots was originally used to make them. Humans aren't the only animals to enjoy mallow plants, and their leaves are a host food for the painted lady butterfly, some moths, the mallow flea beetle and a number of weevils.

Plum, shiso and hibiscus shrub

A shrub is a sweet, slightly acidic syrup made by combining fruit and vinegar. You can serve it mixed with soda water (club soda) or in a cocktail. I make shrubs the slow way, but there is a quick stovetop method if you're in a hurry. A good rule of thumb for shrubs is equal parts fruit, honey or sugar to vinegar.

Add 185 g (6½ oz/1 cup) chopped plums, 25 g (1 oz/½ cup) shiso leaves, 15 g (½ oz/¼ cup) dried hibiscus, and 350 g (12¼ oz/1 cup) raw honey or 220 g (7¾ oz/1 cup) sugar to a clean jar. Crush the ingredients with the end of a wooden spoon, then refrigerate the covered jar for a few days. Stir the mixture every day to evenly coat the fruit and herbs with honey.

When the mixture is ready the fruit should be bathed in an unctuous syrup. Strain out the fruit and herbs using a fine-mesh sieve, and add 60 ml (2 fl oz/¼ cup) apple cider vinegar at a time, adjusting to taste. I like my shrubs quite tart, so I add about 250 ml (8½ fl oz/1 cup) in total. (You can use Lilac vinegar from page 35 instead of apple cider vinegar, though note homemade vinegars are generally more mellow than commercial so you may need to use more.) As the shrub ages, the flavour of the vinegar will mellow.

You can consume your shrub straight away, but a little patience will reward you with a more complex beverage. Store in the refrigerator for up to 12 months.

Begonia

BEGONIA SPP. ——————— BEGONIACEAE

Begoniaceae is a plant family of more than 2040 species. Native to tropical and subtropical climates, the flowers of the genus *Begonia* are a globally popular shade plant. Many species and cultivars of begonia are edible. Wax begonia flowers, which are commonly pink or orange, grow on short red stems that emerge from waxy, deep green leaves. The flowers of tuberous begonias are more densely petalled and resemble a rose. The petals of the flower are characteristically hardy, almost similar to a succulent. Begonia flowers are generally eaten fresh in order to relish their slightly lemony zest and satisfying crunch.

Cross-pollination with a paintbrush

While begonias are fairly easy to propagate from leaf and stem cuttings, I've recently been drawn into the tediously slow but magical world of creating new hybrid begonia seeds by cross-pollinating different species. This process spans months and is only for the most passionate of plant lovers and certainly not for the impatient. It has taken me *many* attempts to sprout viable seeds, but I am hooked and a little high on the idea of creating something new. I have a small collection of about forty-five of my beloved begonias, but you only need one or two flowering plants to begin! Here is how to join me on this journey.

Begonias have both male and female flowers on the same plant. The female flowers have a three-winged ovary at the base of the tepals, making them noticeably different from the males. The male flowers generally open first, so you may need to collect and store their pollen until the females are ready for pollination. To do this, select a male flower that has been open for 1–3 days and carefully collect the yellow pollen from the stamen. Store it in a container in the fridge for up to a month. If you happen to have male and female flowers open simultaneously, carefully smoosh the male stamen onto the female stigma. It doesn't take much force to ensure pollination, so be gentle.

The best time to pollinate a female flower is 24 hours after it opens. You can do this with your stored pollen using a paintbrush, once again being very gentle. I recommend tipping the stored pollen out onto black paper first, to make it easier to see. Don't be afraid to re-pollinate if there is any doubt of success. If pollination is achieved, the ovary will appear darker in the centre of the pod where the seeds form. The seeds are ready to harvest when the pedicel (the small stem connecting the flower to the inflorescence) dries out. This could take around a month. Healthy seeds appear round, plump and amber in colour, and are very, very tiny.

You can store the seeds, or I've had success sowing them in a small, clear plastic container with a lid and a small amount of seed-raising mix, kept consistently moist under a grow light. The seeds will take around a month to sprout. Perhaps you will have created a new hybrid!

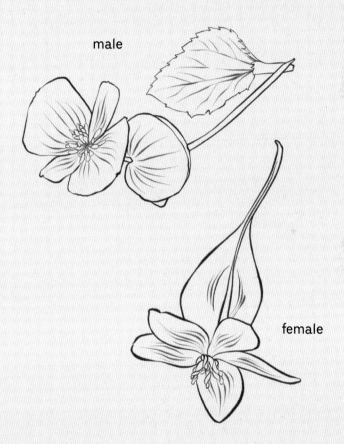

male

female

Hyssop

HYSSOPUS OFFICINALIS —————— LAMIACEAE

Native to Europe and the Middle East, the hyssop plant is named in the Bible, although there is now debate as to which plant was actually meant in psalm 51:7: 'Purge me with hyssop, and I shall be clean.' Hyssop was used for religious purification in Egypt, where priests used to eat it with bread in order to make it suitable for their austere diet.

The fresh herb is an ingredient in the Middle Eastern mix za'atar, but the leaves have a bitter, minty taste, so it is used sparingly. It is also used to flavour absinthe, liqueurs, including Chartreuse, and is used as a fragrance in soaps. The plant is favoured by beekeepers for the rich, aromatic honey its pollen produces. Bees are among the main pollinators of hyssop, as well as other insects and butterflies. It has been used in traditional herbal medicine due to its purported properties as an antiseptic, cough reliever and expectorant.

Nectarine and hyssop sorbet

This easy sorbet is the perfect dessert for late summer. Peel 8 ripe nectarines, remove the pits and chop the fruit. In a blender, purée the chopped nectarine, 1 tablespoon lemon juice and 2 tablespoons chopped hyssop flowers until smooth. Stir in a couple of teaspoons of sugar to taste and blend again. Chill the nectarine mixture in the refrigerator, then freeze in an ice-cream freezer according to the manufacturer's instructions.

Chrysanthemum

CHRYSANTHEMUM SPP. ———————— ASTERACEAE

With masses of long-lasting colour on so many varieties, chrysanthemums are popular cut flowers as well as having cultural significance and medicinal use. In parts of Europe the flowers are only used at funerals, while elsewhere they are gifts for happy occasions such as Mother's Day, and in East Asia they symbolise adversity or grief.

From the original thirty-eight wild species, chrysanthemums have been bred since the eighth century, when cultivation began in Japan, to enlarge the flower size or create new colours. More than 500 cultivars were recorded in 1630 and that number is now well over 20,000.

In China, where most of the original species are found, the plant is venerated as one of four key floral motifs favoured in art (along with plum blossom, orchids and bamboo). It is especially associated with the Double Ninth Festival, which falls on the ninth day of the ninth month – an auspicious date when cleansing activities are embraced, including drinking chrysanthemum tea. There is a similar celebration in Japan, known as Choyo, with a custom called *kiku no kisewata* (covering the chrysanthemum with cotton): gardeners place a pinch of cotton on the centre of the flowers the day before the festival, and the next day they wipe themselves with the dew soaked in the cotton to bring health.

The plant is also used in traditional Chinese medicine and Ayurvedic medicine to treat conditions ranging from colds, fevers and migraines, to eye irritations, vertigo and skin infections. In Korea, chrysanthemum flowers are used to flavour rice wine. However, you have to be sure you are using the right flower – the insecticide pyrethrum is made from two toxic daisy cousins.

Collecting dew

Chrysanthemums, or *kiku* in Japanese, hold a special place in the hearts of the Japanese people. Revered for their beauty and symbolism, chrysanthemums are often associated with the imperial family, longevity and prosperity. In Japan, the Chrysanthemum Festival (Kiku-no-Sekku) is held annually on the ninth day of the ninth month, celebrating the flower's importance in Japanese culture.

The practice of wrapping chrysanthemum blossoms in cotton to collect dew is a delicate and beautiful ritual that has been passed down through generations. The custom is believed to have originated from a desire to preserve the beauty and purity of the chrysanthemum blossoms, as well as to collect the dew that forms on their petals. Dew is considered to be a symbol of purity and freshness in Japan, often associated with the start of a new day.

In the early morning hours, just before sunrise, practitioners of this tradition carefully wrap each chrysanthemum blossom in soft, white cotton. This is done to ensure the dew remains undisturbed on the petals, allowing it to be gently absorbed. The process is slow and meditative, requiring patience and fostering a deep connection with nature.

Once the dew has been collected, the cotton-wrapped chrysanthemum blossoms are carefully unwrapped, revealing the glistening dewdrops trapped within the cotton fibres. The dew is then carefully squeezed from the cotton and collected.

The collected chrysanthemum dew is believed to possess spiritual properties that can cleanse the soul and bring good fortune. It is also thought to have healing properties, making it a highly sought-after elixir. In traditional Japanese medicine, it is used to treat a variety of ailments, including fever, fatigue and inflammation. It is also believed to promote longevity and overall wellness. Some even use the dew as a beauty treatment, applying it to the skin to achieve a youthful and radiant glow.

The tradition of wrapping chrysanthemum blossoms in cotton to collect dew represents the harmonious relationship between humans and nature in Japan. The ritual highlights the beauty and power of the natural world, and the importance of its preservation and appreciation. As modern life becomes increasingly hectic, this ancient custom serves as a reminder of the value of slowing down, connecting with nature, and embracing the wisdom of generations past.

Autumn

Sweet autumn clematis

CLEMATIS TERNIFLORA ——————— RANUNCULACEAE

**This member of the buttercup family carries us into early
autumn (or fall) on a wafting mist of perfume – a trait
for which it is named – with notes of vanilla, jasmine and
almond tantalising the noses of humans, bumblebees and
hawkmoths alike. I'd love to try extracting this generous
scent, which seems heaviest on a warm afternoon and
well into the evening, with the enfleurage method on
pages 136–7.**

Native to Japan and China, this voracious vine in its full glory
is covered in hundreds if not thousands of syrupy, star-shaped
flowers. While each flower is only a diminutive collection of
four petals, the cumulative effect is beguiling, a dramatic
cascade of botanical froth.

The vine has a second flush of beauty once the blooms fade.
Each of the flower's white pistils will elongate, forming a
single seed attached to plume-like hair, giving the effect of
soft, downy fur on the vine. The silvery seed heads add a
diaphanous beauty to the autumn landscape. The seed type,
known by botanists as an achene, is adept at being carried
along gently by the wind and is common in the unrelated
daisy family.

The genus name *Clematis* comes from the Ancient Greek
klema meaning 'twig', 'sprout' or 'tendril'. Don't be fooled
by the delicate appearance of this climber's sweetly scented
flowers and fluffy seeds; this fast-growing plant is tough and
prone to taking over. Few insect pests bother it, deer won't eat
it (although goats may), and it's been declared a weed in New
Zealand (where it was once so popular it was commemorated
on a one dollar note in 1967), and many US states (where it's
been known to pull down telephone poles!).

On the beauty of a seed head

Cut flowers are often discarded when they wilt, but out in the garden flowers continue to serve a natural purpose long after they've finished blooming. The seed heads of dried flowers become food for wildlife and add new layers of depth and colour to garden beds – something to keep in mind when you're thinking about cutting your plants back for winter. If you let nature take its course, the seeds will be dispersed in your garden for the next season, and when new growth comes through in spring it will be sheltered by the dead and dried-out stalks, which are beautiful in their own way.

Saffron

CROCUS SATIVUS ———————— IRIDACEAE

The purple-flowered *Crocus sativus* that blooms in autumn is not to be confused with autumn crocus (*Colchicum autumnale*), which is actually a poisonous plant in the Colchicaceae family with similar flowers. A saffron crocus bulb only produces a single flower, and three thread-like red-orange stigmas attached to the style (the female reproductive part) are harvested from each flower by hand. Between 70,000 to 80,000 are needed to yield 450 g (1 lb) of spice – justification for its status as the world's most expensive spice. Luckily, just a pinch will add saffron's essence to a large pot of rice.

It is considered an essential ingredient in such famous dishes as paella in Spain, risotto in Italy and bouillabaisse in France. It is also widely used in Middle Eastern cooking. In fifteenth-century Venice, then the centre of saffron trade, a special police force was charged with inspecting the wares of saffron merchants to ensure that the saffron was not adulterated. Today this quality control is overseen by the International Organization for Standardization, who use techniques to document the aroma 'fingerprint'. *Crocus sativus* also has a long history of medicinal use dating back to ancient Egypt.

How to grow saffron

As saffron is such a beautiful but expensive spice, consider growing your own if you have enough space! Saffron plants need well-draining soil and lots of sun to avoid rot, but otherwise they are not fussy. In autumn or early spring, plant your saffron crocus bulbs in the ground at about 7.5–13 cm (3–5 in) deep and at least 15 cm (6 in) apart. Once planted, they don't require a lot of care. Fertilise them once a year, and water them if your area doesn't get much rainfall, taking care not to overwater them.

You will need roughly 50–60 saffron flowers to collect 1 tablespoon of spice, but saffron crocuses multiply quickly – in a few years' time you will have many more than you started with.

Goldenrod

Roadsides erupting in gold, signalling the end of summer, are often how Europeans and Americans experience the blossoming of goldenrod. The plant was brought west from the Middle East in the sixteenth century as a cure-all; its Latin name *Solidago* meaning 'to make whole'.

Learning from plants

Naturalist Robin Wall Kimmerer was inspired to study botany because she wanted to understand the magic of why asters and goldenrod look so beautiful together. Why do they tend to grow together, she wondered, a happenstance of stunning complementary gold and purple. She was told this was not science, not the work of a botanist, and that if she wanted to study beauty she should go to art school. Kimmerer was dismayed that conventional botany simply reduces plants to objects – there was no room for the way someone like her thought, marvelling in the beauty of the natural world. In her incredible book *Braiding Sweetgrass*, Kimmerer describes how Indigenous knowledge complements scientific enquiry. She has built a career that honours her Potawatomi heritage, showing how we can enter into a state of reciprocity with nature, and how turning our attention towards the joy that plants bring can heal us and nature in turn. As it turns out, there is a scientific explanation for her commonly observed coupling: the striking complementary colours of aster and goldenrod increase the likelihood of pollination.

Camellia

CAMELLIA JAPONICA ———— THEACEAE

The most magnificent flower of the Theaceae family, *Camellia japonica* is one of between eighty to several hundred (the number is debated) flowering evergreen shrubs in the mystical *Camellia* genus, and the ornamental sister to *Camellia sinensis*, whose leaves we use to make tea.

Camellia cultivation began in China some 2500 years ago. Legend has it that in 2737 BCE, a gentle wind blew *Camellia sinensis* leaves into Emperor Shennong's boiling water. In a fateful act of curiosity, he drank the water and experienced the first historically recorded caffeine buzz. *Camellia sinensis* essentially went on to take over the world. After water, tea is the most popular drink on the planet. Over the last few hundred years, *Camellia sinensis* has been systematically bred to enhance the taste of its stimulating leaves, whereas *Camellia japonica* has been cultivated solely for its five- or six-petalled flowers.

Camellias bloom early, often in late winter, so are nicknamed 'the rose of winter'. With glossy leaves and picture-perfect cold-season blooms, it feels natural that the camellia family became a deeply symbolic icon in its native China, Korea and Japan. It found value as an offering to the gods, and became the muse of poets and artists. In China the flower symbolises the union between two lovers. The petals represent the woman, and the calyx (the leafy part that keeps the petals together) represents the man. The two are bonded together through life and death. Love for the plant is now global; no fewer than seven US cities are nicknamed 'Camellia City'.

Coco's camellia

The camellia became an emblem of Coco
Chanel (1883–1971), her lucky charm and a
signature of her brand – it was embroidered
onto Chanel blouses, pinned onto dresses,
coats and suits, or printed onto fabrics.
The flower's perfect roundness and pure
white petals appealed to Chanel, and the
lack of fragrance meant they would not
overpower her perfume! She was also
attracted to the bloom's androgynous
and provocative status, having been
favoured by both prostitutes and
young men. The love of her life,
Arthur 'Boy' Capel, is said to have
gifted her camellias. Karl Lagerfeld
continued the tradition when he was
creative director of the brand,
reimagining the camellia as part
of every Chanel collection.

Winter

Vanilla orchid

VANILLA PLANIFOLIA ——————— ORCHIDACEAE

A climbing orchid, native to Central American tropical rainforests – where it can grow some 30 metres (98 ft) high using a tree for support – vanilla is the second most expensive spice in the world (saffron being the first). Of all orchid species, within a family of tens of thousands, vanilla is the only one that is considered edible, or that is regularly consumed. Vanilla, unlike its showier cousins, has flowers in restrained shades of yellow, cream and pale green that smell subtly of cinnamon.

Vanilla planifolia, like most orchids, is very difficult to cultivate in any commercial quantity – which is part of why vanilla is inextricably linked to slavery, colonialism and capitalism. The sweet, intoxicating flavour and fragrance of the plant disguises a dark history and indeed present. Until the nineteenth century the main source of vanilla was in Mexico, where the Indigenous Aztecs cultivated it to flavour their ceremonial cocoa. But now the largest grower in the world is Madagascar – an island whose climate and poverty suit the painstaking manual process of vanilla production.

Under cultivation, vanilla is trained on low trees or wooden frames and pruned to encourage flowering, which occurs for only a few hours; pollination must happen during this brief window. Vanilla is generally believed to be pollinated in the wild by a single small type of stingless Mexican bee and potentially native hummingbirds. Everywhere else, if vanilla is to produce pods, each flower must be artificially and individually pollinated by hand.

The pollination technique that is still used today was developed in 1841 by Edmond Albius, a twelve-year-old boy born into slavery in Réunion in the Indian Ocean. A sliver of bamboo is used to pierce the membrane separating the male and female parts of the flower and pollen is transferred by squeezing the two parts gently together, known as 'consummating the marriage'. Within a day the thick green base of the flower swells, and over nine months it matures into a thin pod the length of a hand.

When the yellowing pods are finally plucked, they are disappointingly unscented, and turning them into the familiar rich brown, headily fragrant spice requires yet more laborious effort. After being blanched in boiling water, they are spread out in the sun and wrapped and sweated each night for two weeks, before being dried and cosseted for several more months. During this long process, enzymes create vanillin, the main flavour constituent, and a blend of hundreds of other aromatic molecules.

Crème caramel

Preheat the oven to 140° (285°F) and combine 150 g (5¼ oz/⅔ cup) caster (superfine) sugar with 100 ml (3½ fl oz/⅓ cup) cold water in a pan on medium heat until the sugar dissolves and caramelises, being careful not to burn it. When it is ready, quickly pour the caramel into one large or a few small ramekins, coating the base and sides. Place in a roasting tin and put aside to set.

Whisk together 2 teaspoons orange blossom water (make orange blossom water following the method for Aqua flora on page 53), 200 ml (7 fl oz/¾ cup) full-cream (whole) milk and 350 ml (12 fl oz/1⅓ cups) thick cream (double/heavy). In a separate bowl, whisk together 2 eggs and 4 additional egg yolks with another 75 g (2¾ oz) caster (superfine) sugar as well as ¼ teaspoon vanilla essence.

Slowly pour the cream mixture over the egg mixture while whisking them together, then pour the custard into the ramekin(s) and bake for 1 hour. Leave it to cool then chill in the refrigerator for 1 hour to firm up before running a knife around the edge of the ramekin(s) and turning the crème caramel out to serve.

Witch-hazel

HAMAMELIS VIRGINIANA ——————— HAMAMELIDACEAE

On a damp, midwinter day in a leafless cool-climate garden, the sweet, spicy scent of witch-hazel flowers is a joy – and often a surprise when the source is tracked down to such unremarkable, spidery shapes in yellow, orange or red.

The spindly shrub or small tree is native to eastern China, Japan and the east coast of the United States, where early colonisers learned from First Nations people to use the leaves and bark as a poultice to treat skin conditions, insect bites and poison ivy stings. By the 1840s a small industry was established selling witch-hazel distillation, and it's still sold as an over-the-counter treatment today.

The name 'wych' or 'witch' relates to the Old English word for 'pliant' rather than referring to magic; it was so named due to the bendy quality of the wood, which was apparently used for divining rods to source underground water. It is pollinated in the United States by insects and winter-active owlet moths, which can heat themselves up on cold nights by shivering.

Pharmacopoeia

We are intertwined with the natural world that surrounds us in many more ways than we might first consider. The deep connection between our physical and mental health and nature is well known. But nature and flowers can quite directly save our lives. Around 11 per cent of essential drugs, according to the World Health Organization, originate from angiosperms and many more are derived from plants without flowers. These plant compounds serve as the foundation for powerful medications combating ailments like cancer, Parkinson's and malaria.

For millennia, humans have employed the healing magic of plants to cure various ailments, predating written language.

Witch-hazel can be found in a variety of over-the-counter skin care products, such as toners, cleansers and moisturisers, and is commonly used to treat skin conditions such as acne, eczema and psoriasis. It is also used as a natural remedy for insect bites, cuts and bruises. In addition to topical uses, the tannins in witch-hazel flowers have astringent properties, which can help to reduce inflammation and swelling in the digestive tract.

Researchers often look to natural sources, including flowers, to discover new compounds that may have therapeutic potential. For example, the Madagascar periwinkle (*Catharanthus roseus*) is the source of two important anti-cancer drugs: vinblastine and vincristine. Vincristine has helped increase the chance of surviving childhood leukaemia from 10 per cent to 90 per cent, while vinblastine is used to treat Hodgkin's disease.

Snowdrops (*Galanthus* spp.), while beautiful, were used by the ancient Greeks for their mind-altering effects, and a compound from their bulbs, galantamine, aids in managing Alzheimer's and HIV.

Many of us have benefited from pain-relief medications rooted in specialised plants – one such example is aspirin, originally extracted from willow tree bark, renowned for its pain-relief properties. Although salicylic acid, its active ingredient, is now synthesised, aspirin offers potential benefits like heart attack prevention and cancer treatment.

Flowers also play an important role in traditional medicine. In many cultures, flowers are used to treat a variety of ailments, from minor skin irritations to more serious illnesses. Chamomile flowers have been used for centuries to treat anxiety, insomnia and digestive disorders, while elderflowers are used to treat colds and flu.

Primrose

PRIMULA VULGARIS ——————— PRIMULACEAE

Wild primroses are a staple plant of the romantic English cottage garden, where low mounds of its simple, pale-yellow flowers contrast with taller bluebells. Its name derives from the Latin *prima rosa*, or 'first rose', because its fragrant flowers emerge early – in mild years, soon after Christmas – in woodlands and meadows from the Caucasus and northern Africa right across Europe. The subtle tones of the wild varieties contrast with the gaudy brightness of some human-bred cultivars; those with multiple flowers on each stalk are called polyanthus.

Primrose seeds are spread by ants in a reciprocal arrangement called myrmecochory. The seeds have a fleshy attachment that ants eat. Ants carry them underground to feed their larvae, then the leftover seed is moved to the ants' rubbish area, where it will germinate when conditions are right, fertilised by a handy pile of ant poo. Charles Darwin studied the flowers and discovered a clever form of pollination, aided by two different arrangements of the sexual parts of flowers on separate plants – not quite male and female but complementary all the same. Butterflies, wasps, bees, beetles and flies also pollinate primroses.

Sugar flowers

Both primrose flowers and leaves can be consumed, but it's advisable to avoid them if you are pregnant or taking anticoagulant medication. Sugar flowers serve as exquisite cake and dessert decorations – opt for primroses or other edible blossoms like pansies or violets.

Whisk 1 egg white in a small bowl. Working gently, one flower at a time, paint all surfaces of the blossom with the egg using a small paintbrush, or alternatively, if they are sturdier blooms, you can dip the flowers in the bowl using tweezers. Sprinkle with caster (superfine) sugar or icing (confectioners') sugar. Carefully place the flowers on a tray lined with baking paper and leave at room temperature until they are dry. The flowers can be stored in an airtight container for up to a month.

Daphne

DAPHNE ODORA ———————— THYMELAEACEAE

You can smell the garden where a daphne is growing long before you see the small shrub covered in pinky-white flowers. The spicy sweet scent is quite addictive, but don't go adding it to your salads – all parts of this adorable plant are highly toxic, especially the berries, which will burn your mouth and could be fatal for a child or pet; even the sap can irritate the skin. For most people, carefully cutting a few stems to have indoors is perfectly safe and a lovely way to enjoy this evergreen beauty, but for odour-sensitive people even this can be an allergen. Daphne is found across Eurasia and northern Africa, and is used in traditional medicine in China, Tibet, Korea and the Middle East.

Taking cuttings

It is quite incredible that cut plant stems can grow into brand-new plants. For many plants, as long as they are actively growing, you can take stem cuttings any time and they will grow their own roots. However, it's best to cut woody plants (such as shrubs) at certain times in their growing cycle, so do some research and experimenting based on the plant you'd like to take a cutting from. Some soft-stemmed plants will grow roots in just a glass of water!

Take cuttings early in the morning, when plants have the most moisture. Make a clean cut with a sharp blade from a section of healthy growth. Remove any leaves on the bottom half of the shoots. Keep the cuttings cool and damp until you're ready to plant them, but try to plant them quickly, using moist potting mix and a container with good drainage. You can also invest in a rooting hormone to help your cuttings' success, and create a makeshift greenhouse using a plastic bag around your pot. Keep the plant in bright, indirect sunlight; it should take a month or two for the cuttings to root and be ready to plant in your garden!

All year round

Ylang-ylang

CANANGA ODORATA —————— ANNONACEAE

The essential oil ylang-ylang is well known for its heavy, sweet floral scent and features in many popular perfumes, including Chanel No. 5, but the plant it comes from is less well known. The oil is extracted from the unusual-looking long, drooping flowers – which turn from green to yellow when mature – of the tropical tree *Cananga odorata*, which grows widely from South-East Asia to north-eastern Australia and most of the islands in between. The common name is derived from the Tagalog word for tree, *ilang-ilang*, a reference to the tree's wilderness habitat.

Ylang-ylang is related to the tropical fruit custard apple, and the scented flowers are used in Micronesia and Polynesia for garlands. In Java, the fresh flowers are pounded into a paste to treat asthma, and the dried flowers are used to treat malaria. The black seeds are important food for many rainforest animals. It has been used as a food flavouring and was the key ingredient in the popular nineteenth-century men's hair treatment Macassar oil; however, it is also an allergen and has been removed from some cosmetics.

The principal component responsible for ylang-ylang's sweet fragrance is linalool, a compound found in many plants including lavender, cinnamon and cannabis. It is used in over half of commercially available soaps, lotions and shampoos.

The art of layering scents

Mixing different floral scents to create a perfume is a creative process that requires some knowledge of fragrance families, scent notes and blending techniques.

Understanding the fragrance families is the first step to composing your own perfume using floral scents. There are four main fragrance families: floral, oriental, woody and fresh. Floral fragrances are the most common, and they can be further divided into subcategories like rose, jasmine and lily of the valley. Understanding these fragrance families will help you choose complementary scents.

Pick your base notes first. These are the foundation of a fragrance and are usually made up of woody, earthy or musky scents. Some popular base notes for floral perfumes include sandalwood, vanilla and amber.

Next, select your middle notes. The middle notes are the heart of a fragrance and are usually made up of floral scents like rose, jasmine and ylang-ylang. Choose middle notes that complement each other and your base notes.

To round off the perfume, pick your top notes. These are the first scents you smell when you spray a fragrance and are usually fresh, citrusy or fruity. They're also the first scents to dissipate, so choose top notes that will complement your middle and base notes. Some popular top notes for floral perfumes include bergamot, lemon and grapefruit.

Don't be afraid to experiment with blending. To start blending your floral scents, try mixing a few drops of each essential oil on a blotter or a cotton ball. See how the scents work together, and adjust the ratios until you find a combination you like. Don't forget to write down how you make your blend, including the ratios you used, so you can recreate it later.

Once you've created a blend you like, test it on your skin. Perfume smells different on different people, so make sure you like the way it smells on you. Wear it for a day to see how it develops over time.

You can refine and tweak your blend until you find a combination and balance you love. It may take several tries to get the perfect fragrance, but it's worth it to have a perfume that's uniquely yours.

Acknowledgements

Making a book is no small feat, and this one has been no exception to that rule. It has had the help of so many hands at Hardie Grant Books, all of whom I owe a large debt of gratitude for getting it across the line. The patience, kindness and grace afforded to me by them during this project has been extraordinary.

Eternal thanks as always to my incredibly loving and supportive family, particularly my mother and father, Sally and Bryan Picker. I am incredibly lucky to have such a supportive community of friends surrounding me – Tobias Robinson, Rebecca Castle, Scott Robinson, Matthew Swieboda, Lillian McKnight, Apollonia Swieboda, Silvana Azzi Heras, Pauline Georges, Madeline Dore, Anouk Colantoni, Uli Beutter Cohen, Anna Westcott, Emma Gonzalez, Alanna Greco and Melissa Shannon – without whom I would not have completed this project. I know of nothing worth having more in this world than friendship.

About the author

Adriana Picker is an Australian-born illustrator who currently lives in Sydney, Australia. At the heart of her work is a lifelong passion for flowers, which she manages to find wherever she goes. As an illustrator, artist and designer, she has worked across the diverse fields of publishing, fine arts, film and advertising.

Blossom is Adriana's fifth book. She previously illustrated *Petal: The World of Flowers Through an Artist's Eye*; *The Cocktail Garden: Botanical Cocktails for Every Season*; *Where the Wildflowers Grow: A Botanical Wonderland of Colouring for Adults*; and *The Garden of Earthly Delights: A Lush Wonderland of Colouring for Adults*.

References

Around the World in 80 Plants by Jonathan Drori

The Art of Fermentation: An In-Depth Exploration of Essential Concepts and Processes from Around the World by Sandor Ellix Katz

The Botany of Desire: A Plant's-Eye View of the World by Michael Pollan

Braiding Sweetgrass: Indigenous Wisdom, Scientific Knowledge and the Teachings of Plants by Robin Wall Kimmerer

Green Thoughts: A Writer in the Garden by Eleanor Perényi

growforagecookferment.com

Homebrewed Vinegar: How to Ferment 60 Delicious Varieties by Kirsten K. Shockey

Life in the Garden by Penelope Lively

The Lost Language of Plants: The Ecological Importance of Plant Medicine to Life on Earth by Stephen Harrod Buhner

Nose Dive: A Field Guide to the World's Smells by Harold McGee

Orchid Fever: A Horticultural Tale of Love, Lust and Lunacy by Eric Hansen

Plant Families: A Guide for Gardeners and Botanists by Ross Bayton and Simon Maughan

Practical Botany for Gardeners: Over 3000 Botanical Terms Explained and Explored by Geoff Hodge

The Reason for Flowers: Their History, Culture, Biology, and How They Change Our Lives by Stephen Buchmann

Rootbound: Rewilding a Life by Alice Vincent

The Well Gardened Mind: Rediscovering Nature in the Modern World by Sue Stuart-Smith

Wild Colour: How to Make and Use Natural Dyes by Jenny Dean

The Wildcrafting Brewer: Creating Unique Drinks and Boozy Concoctions from Nature's Ingredients by Pascal Baudar

Index

___

Published in 2024 by Hardie Grant Books, an imprint of Hardie Grant Publishing

Hardie Grant Books (Melbourne)
Wurundjeri Country
Building 1, 658 Church Street
Richmond, Victoria 3121

Hardie Grant Books (London)
5th & 6th Floors
52–54 Southwark Street
London SE1 1UN

hardiegrant.com/books

Hardie Grant acknowledges the Traditional Owners of the Country on which we work, the Wurundjeri People of the Kulin Nation and the Gadigal People of the Eora Nation, and recognises their continuing connection to the land, waters and culture. We pay our respects to their Elders past and present.

A catalogue record for this book is available from the National Library of Australia

Blossom
ISBN 978 1 74379 863 8

10 9 8 7 6 5 4 3 2 1

Publishers: Emily Hart, Pam Brewster
Managing Editor: Loran McDougall
Project Editors: Antonietta Melideo, Claire Davis
Editors: Meaghan Amor, Bonnee Crawford
Design Manager: Kristin Thomas
Designers: Ngaio Parr, Celia Mance
Head of Production: Todd Rechner

Colour reproduction by Splitting Image Colour Studio
Printed in China by Leo Paper Products LTD.

The paper this book is printed on is from FSC®-certified forests and other sources. FSC® promotes environmentally responsible, socially beneficial and economically viable management of the world's forests.

FSC
www.fsc.org
MIX
Paper | Supporting
responsible forestry
FSC® C020056